CUT IT OUT!

Getting Your Head Straight
In Network Marketing

GABRIEL SEDLAK

CUT IT OUT!

Getting Your Head Straight In Network Marketing

Holley, My darling wife, I dedicate this book to you. My coffee buddy, the one I dream with, the one I gaze at the stars with, you mesmerize me every minute of every day. Thank you for always believing in me.

Introduction

I t's hard to see in muddy water. Put ten network marketers with ten different companies in a room, and they'll all believe theirs is the best. They will tell you they have the greatest science, unprecedented positioning, record breaking growth, never before seen technology, the most cutting edge compensation plan in the industry, the timing couldn't be better, and that they're *the* company to join. Classic my daddy can beat up your daddy scenario. Hey, I get it.

I started in the industry at 18. I turned 48 at the writing of this book, and those kinds of statements have been boldly declared by companies and consultants for as long as I can remember. Our industry does in fact provide the best of the best in products, services, and opportunities. But we must remember that real long-term, sustainable success — which is the goal — comes from having the right mindset and choosing to personally operate with excellence and integrity no matter what. In addition to and not seperate from that, success comes from representing companies that transcend the latest product fads and opportunity du jour. Many "opportunities" roll in like waves, and after a bit, just like waves, they roll back out.

This industry is about change. It's about offering incredible products while working to create time freedom, life freedom, and financial increase with you in control in the drivers seat. Is it hard work? You better believe it, but SOOO worth it! This industry is the great equalizer for anyone who engages properly. Where else can anyone from any background have the *potential* to create for massive change for their families, without a nine foot resume?

Long-term sustainability is *everything* and needs to be fought for and guarded. Don't risk following those who go from opportunity to opportunity every two years, always promising greener grass and touting the new venture as the greatest thing ever. Didn't they say that about the last one? Pulling teams along from deal to deal is all too common in network marketing — and way too destructive!

Even if greener grass is promised, you can't just take it. You still have to create your own green grass. When you show up to get the promised green grass, you are handed a bag of seeds. That can be quite the awakening!

Ask the tough questions. Not all opportunities are created equal. Not all soil is good ground, regardless of who is saying it is. We all start off with a bag of seeds. Plant the same seed in two different patches of land and each one will grow differently. Differences in soil, the types of seeds that are being planted, and how those seeds are cultivated by the farmer all impact the outcome of the harvest. The same is true in network marketing.

Ask yourself the tough questions too. Are you really going to work your business faithfully? Or are you going to throw it at the wall and hope it sticks? If it sticks, great. If not, then off you go to the next opportunity?

Has your desire to be "first" and "groundfloor" — as though that's the only way success is obtained in an opportunity — caused you to drink one of the strongest elixirs that consistently derails multitudes in our industry? I have watched many people lose everything they built because they dropped what they already had in their hands to grab something new. People are all too quick to diminish what they are doing when a zealous voice seem to always show up when they are hitting a challenging spot in their current opportunity.

Remember how you do anything is how you do everything. Be faithful and treat your opportunity like a career that can change your life in a BIG way, because it can! Be sober minded and extend mercy and grace to yourself and others as you build — this will make any uphill battle far less steep. How do I know these things? Because I have stepped in all of it. And by the grace of God, I shook it off and redirected my habits and the way I was thinking before I could have lost what I gained.

Network marketing is like a rocket. It has the capacity to break the gravitational pull of life that keeps so many from ever going high enough to really experience the vastness of what's out there. When you can really see from that height, you'll never allow circumstances, or people's opinions to stand in the way of you pursuing your dreams.

If you are truly growing your business, you will inevitably sooner or later come to challenging places. Guess what? There's good news! *You* have the power to fix whatever those challenges are. Remember: *You* are the common denominator wherever you go.

I want to help keep you from being your own stumbling block. Use this book like a sword. Swing it at all the contrary forces, especially your own conditioning that has stood in the way of you reaching your dreams for far too long.

If you really desire to be successful in network marketing, then you're going to have to **CUT IT OUT!**

~ Gabriel

CONTENTS

1. BUILDING BLOCKS

Your Sword

I have said the following statement publicly for as long as I can remember. Whether in person, over the phone, on a video chat, or even in front of large gatherings of people...

I did not pray the many years I did to meet the woman of my dreams only to spend the next thirty years away from her. I did not marry her to spend fifty hours a week away from her working for someone else. I did not have children with her only to put them in daycare, or off to school all day only to see them briefly in the morning and a few minutes before bed. Giving them merely emotional crumbs at the end of each day isn't fair or what they deserve. That is not what I signed up for. That is not the American Dream, and that is not my dream! So, I decided to do something about it.

That Statement is **MY SWORD**! Those words cut through everything that tries to block my view, prevent freedom for my family, or choke out what I produce. By swinging it, the weeds and vines that constantly try to grow up and entangle me in life are cut back so I can see clearly what's before me. I hope you will decide to swing your sword. Whether you realize that you have one now or not, you will!

Your Soil

No farmer plants a crop without first considering the harvest. Have you considered the harvest before you planted your seed? Have you considered what sowing the seeds from your future harvests can produce in the future? One ear of corn has approximately 800 kernels. If you sow them, that's 800 plants that have between two and four ears of corn each. Do the math a few times and before you know it, the harvest is immeasurable. From now on as you continue reading, I want you to think about your network marketing business as **leverage** for your future.

Most people get corn and only think of eating it, without any thought of planting. Whatever you do, make sure you settle in your mind that the resources of this world (seeds and harvest) were designed to serve you, but only if planted correctly. With your harvest in mind, I want you to imagine what could you do and accomplish in life if you had that kind of seed power?

Your Rocket

The network marketing industry rewards you for passion, hunger, and fire in your belly — not for what's just on your resume. Now, CEOs of corporations, doctors, professional ball players, or the rich and famous *ultimately* do not have any advantage over you, if you put in the work! Our industry is the great equalizer for those willing to press through until their breakthrough comes. Notice I said *until*! Did I say you will live at their level? Maybe, maybe not, that's up to you, I don't know what's in your heart. I am saying, that this industry has the ability to create the greatest wealth of all....time. When you are rich in time, what else do you really need? It's not only the dollar amount that determines how you will live.

He's Alive!

You've *got* to get this handled sooner rather than later. This is one of the main trainings I regularly teach people when it comes to maintaining or gaining the freedom they desire.

As his creation started to move on the table, Dr. Frankenstein yelled out in surprise, "He's alive!"

Did you know that every few years every cell in your body replaces itself? The old is replaced by the new. Your hair, heart, brain, blood, bones, skin, all the cells from head to toe are replaced to create a "New You." You actually become a new person! Think about this. In the past you went through things, said things, acted on things, had experiences with things, and your old body and mind was there and was the vessel doing them, right? Yes, but that version of you doesn't exist anymore. The old you has been replaced!

Unfortunately, without proper understanding, just like Dr. Frankenstein's monster, the new you is reintroduced to old feelings, emotions, and imagery. When you sew or sow dead things from the past to living things present, you create a monster, and when you bring it to life he starts wrecking things!

> When you sew or sow dead things from the past to living things present, you create a monster, and when you bring it to life he starts wrecking things.
>
> ~ Gabriel Sedlak

It's almost impossible to separate the pieces — so the monster has to be killed. I go in depth on this regularly when I speak, and it's astonishing how many get free from their past when they *see* it! The past has no right to live in the present....especially if it's dead, so don't bring it back to life!

This is a huge key for living abundantly in the now. Don't sew or sow (meaning knit together or plant) yesterday into today, you'll end up creating a monster! If you have, the way to victory is to first and foremost extend grace and forgiveness to yourself. Then be merciless when it comes to getting rid of that monster, and the thoughts that try to creep back in and pretend that they "are you". That is how it works, an unrenewed mind can be tricked into thinking dead things are living.

I heard a teaching on Roman punishment some years ago, and one of the ways the Romans dealt with accused criminals? They would bind a deceased person from the crime to the back of the criminal and force the criminals to walk around with them on their backs. After a while the decay was so advanced that it ate into the living person's body until they died as well.

Graphic I know, but too many of you do this to yourselves all the time! You constantly place the dead things of yesterday — fear, insecurity, shame, moments with all the feelings and imagery — and bind them onto today until you become like the walking dead. You become infected, infested, and ineffective until you can't move forward.

We wonder why so much of our lives never seem to change, why we can't be present and can't seem to shake yesterday. Because the past is still alive, and we allow it. This book will help deliver you from the mindsets that have prevented you from living in the present. Which brings me to the present!

You joined or are considering joining a network marketing company. **This book is addressing that industry, but you'll quickly realize that to limit this book to network marketing would be foolish.** It's about being victorious in life! Wherever you are on your journey, and whatever your goals are, the six inches between your ears can be the longest distance on earth if you let it. Or it can simply be six inches. It's as simple or as difficult as that. Success in this industry and in life really starts to happen when that distance is crossed, and how long it will take is up to you.

If there were a list of the worst mistakes people make that prevent them from experiencing success, at the very top of the list would be: Stop being Dr. Frankenstein.

2. THIEVES

Fruit Is Attacked Or Ignored

One thing that's critical to understand — and is guaranteed in life — is that wherever there is fruit, wherever there is a goodness, wherever there are wonderful things that bring life, there will always be an assault against it.

I remember attempting to grow cherry tomato plants some years ago on the back deck of the second story of a house I was renting. I bought all the pots, soil, seeds, the little plants, fertilizer, and pest control. As the plants began to grow, I noticed the little clear white aphids would show up when the initial flowers started to appear. They would crawl all over the leaves and try to eat the soon-budding tomatoes. Where they came from, I have no idea. They literally seemed to appear out of thin air. After several attempts, I was able to get rid of the aphids using hot peppers that I blended in water then fine strained out the liquid, put it in a spray bottle, then sprayed it all over the plants. It didn't alter the plants or flavor ultimately; it just got rid of the problem naturally. And I was able to salvage most of the plants before they were ruined entirely. Then came the next round of assault. Birds. What was different about this attack was that, day after day, the birds would sit on the fence and just watch. This went on for about a week until the tomatoes do what they do the last hours before they are truly ripe. They suddenly grew a substantial amount that last eight to twelve hours or so. They go from orange, light red, to red, plump, and really ready to eat. *That* final stage is when the birds would swoop down and take them. I later learned that all the really powerful phytonutrients come to life in the final hours of ripening. Ahhhhh! If birds innately know this, then do we not think that the world around us and the forces at work know this?

How many young people full of life and hope are exposed and pushed into things that steal the innocence and defile the mind and body? This sets into motion a pattern of wandering and unfulfilled emptiness. Do I need to say more about that?

There will always be things that attempt to negatively violate. People's opinions will always try to smash anything you build. But try as they may, when you are rooted and grounded in truth, the negativity has *no* foothold. Even if it did, remember that you have access to the truth to remove it quickly and easily. You have the power to keep those thieves from ever coming back.

As the old saying goes, you can't keep the birds from flying above your head, but you sure can keep them from making a nest in your hair!

Of course, this is a Biblical lesson. After the seed is sown, what happens? The birds of the air, the wind, the sun, the lack of water, and the shallow roots try to prevent lasting fruit.

The people who are able to identify the reasons for the fruit not lasting especially after they have worked so hard planting, will be the ones who will be able to continue until their breakthrough happens. What a beautiful harvest awaits those who overcome!

Crabs

According to Wikipedia,

> *"Crab mentality, sometimes referred to as crabs in the bucket, is a phrase that describes a way of thinking best described by the phrase, "If I can't have it, neither can you." The metaphor refers to a pot of crabs. Individually, the crabs could easily escape from the pot, but instead, they grab at each other in a useless "king of the hill" competition, which prevents any from escaping and ensures their collective demise. The analogy in human behavior is that members of a group will attempt to "pull down" (negate or diminish the importance of) any member who achieves success beyond the others, out of envy, conspiracy or competitive feelings."*

I love this definition because it describes a scenario that

we are all faced with and all ultimately must master to be free.

With this introduction in mind, I will walk you through a process that reveals what has been holding you back from success in network marketing and even entrepreneurism in general for that matter. You have one life. I dare you to grab a big sword and cut out all the things that are holding you back!

3. DO PEOPLE KNOW WHAT YOU DO?

L et's start this thing off with the very obvious but easily missed. Since you have decided to be in business for yourself as an entrepreneur or in network marketing specifically, I suggest you simply start off by asking people,

> *"I'd love to share with you what I do, what I'm looking for, and see if you may have an interest in being a part?"*

It's shocking to me, in a world where everything is shared on social media, how many people kind of know what you do, kind of heard about it, maybe, but because of the friendship, what box they keep you in, or what they think of you, they truly have NO idea. People can *like* you but not *respect* you. This lack of respect often prevents people from being open to learning about your opportunity because they think what in the world do *you* know about X,Y, or Z? There are many reasons people can't — or won't — hear you. Do you know what I think the most likely reason is? You just flat-out have never clearly and concisely shared what you do with them. It's that simple and that obvious, but never really addressed.

Shocker I know! But most people never take this clear and direct approach. Do you know how refreshing it is for you to be direct, clear, honest, and forthright with your intentions and not the vague indirect approach with the eventual wind up to the ask? I hate that tactic, and NEVER do it. If you can't just say it clearly, then something is wrong. This is one of the reasons people many times resist opportunities — because all too often messengers play games.

When you begin to share with people your opportunity, even if you've been doing it for a while, you'll find the closest people to you are the least informed. You have never just sat them down and shared it clearly. Your friends, your family, and even your spouse many times don't really understand what you do, usually because of the closeness and familiarity, and all the weirdness between people that know you. They definitely don't understand the magnitude of the business model and the potential to have their lives changed because of it. When you do share your opportunity (and when I say "opportunity" I mean the WHOLE message, your products, and your business model) with people, whether close to you or people you've just met, make sure you make your job easier and not harder. Use the resources your company has for you, like a PowerPoint presentation, a video overview presentation, explain your products in detail, and how the business side works, and whatever tools your company has provided. Why? Duplication. Winging it and deviating from the message will only keep you from seeing your business from growing smoothly. If you are scattered, you will develop a scattered team.

If you try to *sell* it, or are great at articulating the message, or have massive experience in the industry, people may feel that they have to have those skills too in order to be successful. But if you walk into the coffee shop, buy someone a coffee, open up your laptop and share a simple message, that is less intimidating. Anybody can do that! *That* is the key to this thing. People want to know one thing: Can I do it? Make sure you don't make it hard for them to become a customer or to join you in business by adding to that very simple process!

This is a critical part of the process and hard for most. People sometimes believe that changing the recipe and baking the cake at 500° for 30 minutes will be better than baking it at 350° for 1 hour. That mentality usually stems from being a bit ashamed or embarrassed with what they are sharing. They act a bit apologetic about the opportunity and add to an otherwise simple process, message, and proven recipe. Ask yourself whether you are even a little bit, a tiny bit apologetic, ashamed, or embarrassed about what you are sharing. If the answer is YES, ask yourself why. Then write down your answer. Once you have that answer, ask yourself why you wrote down that answer, then again write down that answer and ask yourself why you wrote down that answer. Continue to ask why and write down each answer. You'll begin to discover one of the BIG reasons why success seems to slip through your fingers. Exposing and eliminating **that root** through this process, will cause it to never come back again, and if it tries, you'll be able to cut it out!

Exposure Is Key!

Whatever method gets you in front of people...do that! Hopefully you are having coffee meetings a lot, video chats a lot, and hosting frequent in-person gatherings a lot. People who do all of these things on their journey are the people who will ultimately see the most success in our industry. It's that simple. That process is duplicatable and will become a metronome of regular activity people can follow. You and your team don't have to (and shouldn't!) deviate from it. As you get bigger, you may want to look into hiring a professional to help you scale if that makes sense, but there should always be consistent person to person business gatherings regardless of how big you get. Never remove the human element out of it. The responsibility of the message is on the company, simply making you the messenger! Your job is to be the salt on the steak, not the steak. You are a messenger, not the message. As a messenger, you have three jobs:

1. Explain why you joined (your personal story).

2. Tell the simple message of your opportunity,

including the products and the business.

3. Ask what the level of interest is. PERIOD!!!!!

One of the most successful companies in the history of our industry that really helped to create much of what we all enjoy today as network marketing, used the following method. This company had a process to eliminate the noise and force income-producing activities. They would say, "Okay, so you have a specific goal that you want to reach, right? Okay, great. So how many times have you shown the plan this week?"

The funny thing is that the people who "show the plan" meaning sharing the products, and the business model, are the ones who have the most customers, grow the biggest teams, have the most personally sponsored people, and have the biggest checks. By default, the more points of distribution you have (consultants), the more product sales you have (customers). I'm not saying recruit only. You know better than that, absolutely NOT! And if that is the dominant message a company shares, and has the products on the back burner, or as a secondary thought.....RUN! As the messenger, you must cover all the points (the three parts to your job I mentioned previously).

Depending on the answer to the third part (level of interest), you move forward accordingly. Most people will become customers, some will join you in business, and a few will build it big!

To help you understand how to create exponential growth and build big, I want to explain what McDonalds wants. It wants corners with restaurants on them. McDonalds is in the real estate business. The more corners they have, the more burgers that are sold! Starbucks wants coffee shops on corners. The more corners they have coffee shops on, the more coffee they sell. And, yes, they are also in the real estate business.

The real estate broker wants talented realtors in their brokerage firm. The more talented realtors who work for the broker, the more listings are created, and the more homes are sold. You get what I'm saying. Personally sponsoring people, not exclusively, but as part of your message oddly enough, seems to ultimately cures most the ills that this industry or your business could ever throw at you! If you stay focused on that, you'll own a lot of corners and ultimately have exponentially more customers than you could have ever had by yourself.

All of this should make huge sense to us. This is how traditional businesses work. They are constantly interviewing for talented people to work for them. Many are hired. Many leave. Some stay. A few become champions and stay with the company for the long haul. The world knows how to do that already, so why do we treat this business any differently? We cannot treat it like a lottery where you are waiting to find your million-dollar earner as your ticket to success. No company says, "Boy, if we could just hire our Rockstar, our business would be successful."

You've heard stories about somebody who joined an opportunity, went crazy building and their sponsor's business exploded, and suddenly they're "rich". It happens, because they have massive momentum under them. But you can't duplicate or train from that position. (BIG MIS-TAKE!) If it happens, INCREDIBLE, but that is not what everything is hinged on, nor how you should train your teams

Your Rockstars will always come in time, but you can't train and build on the lotto mentality. You have to consistently share the message. The income will start growing and continue to grow if you don't deviate —follow that recipe!

*Coffee meetings: Do lots of them!

*Business/product gatherings at a public locations and/or at your house: Do lots of them!

*Video chats one on one/or with groups of prospects: Do lots of them!

You can hide behind social media and think that is how to build an empire in network marketing. You can potentially grow quick organizations through social media, but sustainability, retention, loyalty, and relationships are glued together by building a person-to-person business. People want to be where they are celebrated. They don't want to only be part of something virtual. Leverage virtual events, absolutely. We live in that world, but don't use them as the *only* means of building. People want to be a part of something and go somewhere where they are known.

Fill your calendar. Host the meetings. Get on video conferences. Get in front of people. I don't care if there's two people there. I don't care if there's 50 people there. If you are doing a in-person meeting don't cater it; your job is not to feed people. Coffee, water, maybe donuts. That's it! When the time comes to do the elaborate stuff and the big venues, great. When you get to that point, do them at a mind-blowing level! But for regular gatherings, keep it simple. Remember what you do duplicates. The harder and more elaborate you make it, the harder it is for the team to follow. Don't spend all kinds of money. Don't over-plan, and don't worry about some flashy office space or hotel. It's a cup of coffee and a conversation. *That* is what sets people free. Do enough of those, and eventually it may just turn into a firestorm that you can't control, and that's a good thing!

By that point, your leaders will have risen up and now it's a group effort. The dynamics create a strong and diverse message that everyone can relate too. Getting your opportunity (product and business model) in front of fresh eyes is your only job. Any other action honestly is just not on the top of the list of being fruitful. There are a million distractions and "good things" to occupy your time that will always try to take the place of getting your message in front of people, don't fall prey to them.

Remember, in the beginning you are grossly underpaid for an enormous amount of work, or at least it feels that way. But after a while you may just be grossly overpaid because of the enormous harvest that is now growing from all the seeds you planted in the beginning!

So, I ask again: How many times have you shown the plan? Are you sharing? Or are you spending all your energy trying to figure out what to tell people or what training to go to? Are you telling everyone that you exhausted all your social media friends? Are you telling yourself the people in your town are different, just don't have the money for the products, or wouldn't do this business? Do you honestly believe you can't find people at all to share your opportunity with?

Are you spending all of your energy trying to come up with some script or trying to talk like one of the power players in your company? All of the above will derail you. Make your message genuine, pure, honest, and simple. Quit thinking you are missing something, need another skill or some special angle before you will see growth. Turn all that off, simply share and shine like only you can. It's THAT simple, though not always easy, but TOALLY possible!

4. DO I SELL THE PRODUCTS OR THE OPPORTUNITY?

GREAT QUESTION..... You'll find that some people get paralyzed by feeling they need to focus heavily on trying to only get customers. They end up making the business a secondary issue, even avoid it, if they even share about it at all. On the other hand, some people are so intense about sharing the business that they make the products a secondary issue, far in the background, not good! Remember: No money changes hands in this industry and into your pocket without customers. It's all about the product, and it's all about the opportunity. They are two sides of the same coin.

So what is the answer?

Again, you are the messenger. Tell the story! Then ask how they want to be involved and plug them in accordingly, I don't "sell" it either way. I support them as my customer if they choose that, and I'm always there to answer any questions they may have. If they choose to be my business partner, I match their effort and encourage them that they are in business for themselves but not by themselves, and find out what they want this business to do for them in their life. Once I find that out, I partner with that.

Here's a great explanation. Have you ever taken a massive amount of change that you've collected to one of those coin machines (usually in grocery stores)? As you slowly begin to pour in the change, the dollar value begins to increase on the screen. It automatically separates the quarters, dimes, nickels, and pennies in the correct slots. At the same time, the machine removes the paper clips, lint balls, M&Ms, foreign currency, or whatever else seems to find itself in your bag. When it's finished, you take the receipt to the cashier and you get the cash. That is how this business works! Tell the company story, why you decided to join. Explain the products and explain the business model. Let the machine do the rest of the work! People will decide where they fit, that is not your job to decide.

Fight the urge to be the expert. Don't allow yourself to get stalled before you can proudly share your opportunity. If you try to have everything figured out first, you'll never start speaking to people. The time for you to start sharing will actually become like a mirage. Like when you're driving on a highway and the closer you get to your destination, it just remains on the road before you in the distance. Success rarely happens after this exhaustive process.

People will tell you this industry doesn't work. They'll say things like, "Yeah, I tried that, but decided it wasn't for me. I just couldn't get it going." Or some people are always getting ready to get ready. They'll tell you their strategy is to do all their research, all their reading, and be able to describe the products at a scientific level. Then they will create a game plan with a few other people. Once they do that, then they will start scheduling meetings and start inviting people.

That is a trap. It sounds intelligent, but it creates a very hard-to-follow process that makes YOU the message. Remember: You are the messenger. Smile and point, like Vanna White on Wheel of Fortune! Just turn letters and ask questions until the audience can read the phrase for themselves.

WARNING: If you try to be the expert first or predetermine what your listeners will choose by limiting what part you share, it will create massive frustration and you won't see your business grow to the level it could have.

Little Victories Are Big Victories

It starts with the little victories. If you are ever to be a great leader, with the healthy balance of giving and receiving and a desire for lasting success in this industry, then receiving is another critical part of the process! I ask the people who are joining me, and those who have already joined me, even if they have been getting paid for a while, "What are you going to do *for yourself* with your next check? I need you to tell me what you are going to do *for you* to reward yourself for working hard and making that check."

Most of the time people can't answer the question. They take a big breath and just stare at me. Oddly enough, this goes for people who have been in the business for a while as well. They still feel guilty, but they have no problem with the giving. I say, "I want you to immediately buy something for yourself when you're paid. It's not about how much you made. If it's $20, $200, $2,000, $20,000, or $200,000 on your check this month, it doesn't matter. I want you to physically identify something that you want."

There is something extraordinarily powerful when you can do something for yourself. It seems to be especially hard for women to self-reward, because they are always serving everyone else. A while back, I was coaching a mix of business women, stay-at-home moms, college students, and retired women. It was literally the perfect blend of people to speak to on this subject. As we were digging deeper into this subject, one lady mentioned that rewarding herself was **THE** hardest part of her business when she started. In the beginning the idea of rewarding herself was foreign, but she agreed to try it even though guilty feelings almost stopped her. So she set out to buy herself a Coach keychain. She felt guilty, thought it unnecessary and frivolous, and it even made her angry to "lower herself" to play this stupid game. She said she came up with a dozen other "smart" uses for the money, even though the keychain was only around $50. She said she stared at it all evening after buying it and wouldn't even put her keys on it for a couple days. She was sure she was going to take it back, and just decided to lie to everyone and say that she loved it. Then it hit her. The pleasure she gained from giving to others, she somehow was able to put that *same feeling* and value on loving herself. As uncomfortable as that was she didn't push off the feeling and actually began to get quite emotional. After a while she realized that her reservations and guilt from even doing the smallest things, came from having huge responsibilities put on her at a young age. It was never OK to think of herself as a priority. That eventually morphed into the idea that anything for *her* was selfish and anything for *them* was love. So she only did for them, even after she grew up and got married, she carried that to a bigger extreme with her family. So she chose to never do for herself, regardless if she needed it or not. She then shared that her resolve became so strong and pure from those feelings that washed over her heart from seeing her value and really loving herself, that she never again would or could be afraid to love herself in what she thought was in an extravagant way! She couldn't wait until the next check and was already thinking about what she'd treat herself to! Guess what the next gift was? A Coach wallet! After she got that, she worked up to her first Coach handbag. Before you knew it, she was at the Michael Kors store. She bought the best one they had just on principle. She said that the handbag was so awesome, and she felt so good buying it with the money *she* earned, that she bought the same handbag for a friend too. She was so grateful and free, which was now her new normal. She mentioned that she had never given a gift like that before, with such a love attached to it for the person she was giving it to, because she was free to do it without obligation. Since then she graduated to Louis Vuitton, then Prada, Chanel, you name it. She's good now!

Are you starting to understand what I'm saying? Receiving is not optional for you. It's mandatory! You've got to be okay with beautiful things. You've got to be okay with excellence. You've got to be okay and be free of your past monsters when the increase comes in your business. I don't want you to pay bills with it only. Do that in addition to rewarding yourself! I don't want you to buy practical things only. I want you to have rewards that offer a sweet cherry on top of *your* hard work. Something you've always wanted, big or small. It's all relative. Every time you glance at it, worth, reward, and love for yourself is poured all over you again. Your labor is valuable and what you're doing really matters. Change is never restricted to one person. Those all around you will be blessed because of your work. Your team needs you to be free in this area. It will help them live abundantly and free as well. You need to verbalize it if you've done something for yourself with the last check. Share it with the team. Tell them how you felt doing it, why it was so hard to do before, and why it's so important to start. As you continue to make a big deal over these rewards, it will become a huge point of celebration for everyone. You'll encourage and empower people because they see you free to both give *and* receive.

It is not unspiritual. It is not wrong to love yourself. Even the scripture mentions loving people must come out of loving yourself first or your love for them isn't complete or pure. I have seen this one point be the breakthrough that changes all the emotional dynamics in someones business. I've seen people skyrocket because now they can be truly abundant. You must be free and celebrate with others in an environment of hope and increase, building each other up to greater things in this life. You don't get a second try at this life, and we must master it!

WARNING: Waiting for a certain dollar amount on your check before you start personally rewarding yourself is one of the traps. Do it NOW no matter what your current check is.

5. BUSINESS IS SLOW BECAUSE OF...

Have you ever heard anybody say very casually and very naturally:

- This is flu season so I'll reach out in a few weeks.

- I need to wait for the kids to get out of school and then I'm going to start reaching out to people.

- This summer people aren't really around and are traveling. Once summer is over, I'll start reaching out again.

- Christmas time is such a crazy time. I'm just going to get through the holiday season and then I'm going to start building my business.

- It's the first of the year, and people need time to get back into the swing of things. I'll reach out around March because people will be ready then.

- Oh, I can't make it at the end of the week. I need more time to plan, and my babysitter needs more notification than a week.

- Friday isn't good for me. How about Thursday? Do you have a meeting then?

- I need to reorganize my sock drawer on that day. So sorry! Maybe next time.

- Hey, I know you are starting your meeting in an hour, but the cat just threw up on the bed and I have to wash the sheets. Let me know the next time you're doing something and maybe I can come then.

- Hey, I spoke to my husband, and he said to ask you what you were going to talk about because there is no need to come if I already heard it. Are you going over anything new?

On and on and on. Endless reasons! But call somebody 30 minutes before you are going to go eat chips and salsa, and they're already in the car on their way to meet you before you hang up!

Because I worked as hard as I did, and I mean WORKED, I was able to bring my wife home over ten years ago form corporate america by the end of our first year in our current opportunity, and we weren't using social media at that time. If I was using that in 2008...please! Myspace was slowing down, and Facebook wasn't really understood yet, at least by me. In our company we only had a few core products, the prior reputation of our founders, and hope. We were big vision casters. We shared why we're going after it and hoped people joined us. But if they didn't, we were still in it, no matter what. There weren't "top earners" back then. There was no car program. We weren't a billion-dollar brand yet. We had no real traction in the market yet. It was what it was, and the beginning was the beginning. I was hungry. I turned off the opinions of people, and I put my head down, and created a level of freedom (which varies from person to person) that allowed me to bring her home, period! I won before I started, and our YES changed countless lives all over the world. It can be the same for you. Your YES will create a snowball effect that will carry a multitude with you.

If you are still in "hoping mode," thinking it sure would be nice if this thing could work out, then you've already nailed your feet to the floor! If you're fine watching everybody else off in the distance succeed, are still having a hard time believing it's okay for you to be successful, but don't have any faith in yourself yet, then use my faith! I know, beyond a shadow of a doubt, you can too, because I know where I was in my mindset when I started in this industry over 30 years ago!

Now take my hand and keep reading. I give you permission to turn off the opinions of people. Turn off the circumstances that temporarily surround you and make you feel that they *are* you. Wrong! They are circumstances, and you are not your circumstances. They may be true, but they are not THE truth. What's going on in your life is temporary, a fog, a mist that prevents you from seeing. You are not your environment, unless you allow it and allow the feelings to crawl in and brainwash

you into thinking so. Because you have the power to create your reality, you will partner with what you believe. That agreement and partnership actually makes what was a mere illusion into substance, a reality.

When you look into the early etymology of the word *circumstance*, which (Lexico) does a great job of explaining, It's easy to see it explained as being encircled around with issues, time limits, situations, people, etc., while you stand in the middle staring at the things surrounding you. Now if you decide to believe these circumstances are the truth, you'll stand paralyzed. Do you know the story of the elephant that has a chain around its leg attached to a post? Eventually it quits trying to pull on it, assuming it's impossible to get free. When the captors eventually remove the chain, the poor elephant remains by the pole and doesn't go anywhere. The saddest part is that the elephant has the power to break the chain and jerk the pole out of the ground at any time. You, my friend, at any time can do that very same thing. You are powerful enough. You are enough. You are not stuck! Knowing that fact is 95% of the battle. The last 5% leaves one remaining question: WILL YOU jerk your imaginary chains out of the ground, or has the familiarity with it caused you to decide to live right there?

WARNING: If you are looking for a reason why your business isn't growing, then you are guaranteed to find one.

The truth is that God gave us the ability to dominate in life. He gave us the keys and gave us the power in our words to change anything. All things are possible to those who believe. The New Testament (His Last Will and Testament) was written with you in mind. You were written in His WILL! Being written in a will matters not, unless you know about it, read it, agree to it, and then take into your hands what was offered in it.

A gift no matter how great, is only an offer unless received.

I give you permission to turn off the noise. I give you permission to abundantly and fearlessly get your opportunity of possibility and hope before people. I give you permission to take this gift, be loud and proud about how it, to stop tiptoeing and telling yourself, "Gosh I don't want to be pushy and try to sell people." WHAT!?! You don't want to be pushy? It's not about pushy. It's about conviction! People will go to your movie, buy your popcorn, buy your coffee cup, wear your T-shirt, and tell you, "I'm so happy for you. Good luck on your business venture. I've been watching you." But they'll never become your customer or join you. You will only be a touchpoint of awareness for them to get one step closer to the person who truly has conviction about the opportunity. Then they will join those people, someone they believe, someone who's CONVICTED!

People cheer and applaud for underdogs but only join "top dogs." Are you a top dog in your mind and in your posture? Or are you apologetic, soft, half-committed, indoctrinated, and trapped in the illusion of circumstances? People will smell the apathy a mile away. For those of you who say you can't get anyone to join you as a customer or in your business, maybe now you have a better understanding as to one of the main reasons why.

The truth doesn't set us free. It's the truth that we know, apprehend, ingest, clothe ourselves with, and walk in that sets us free!

6. NO TIME LIKE THE PRESENT

Opportunity knocks, but we have to answer the door.

It's never the right time for anything. You just do it anyway and adapt! Like having kids, getting married, moving into a new home, having a garage sale, going clothes shopping (a few more pounds off and then you will, right?) Starting a new job, moving to a new state, going on a vacation, going to an opportunity meeting, the list goes on and on. There's always an excuse to not do something.

Do you think that this industry, and specifically your opportunity, is a less noble career choice than a "traditional" job? Have you ever gotten hired and on the first day your new boss says, "Please sit down for a few minutes, we are so thrilled you have joined us. Now we want to introduce you to the whole team." And one by one they introduce themselves and explain how they are there to help you succeed and succeed big. They cannot wait for you to have such great success that you no longer come into the office. They tell you they hope you can even retire early and spend every day with your family pursuing your dreams! They tell you that they will handle all the shipping, handle all the web services, all the e-commerce, and email your customers and consultants to always keep them in the loop. They share that the higher up you get in rank and title, the more money you will make. The more you help others do the same, the more money you will make. Down the road, if you choose, you can even will or sell your business to someone. Have you ever had that experience? I would wager you have not! In THIS INDUSTRY that is EXACTLY what is being said! It is not a lesser pursuit; you have a gift in your hands. It's not a burden. It's not bugging people. It's a gift!

Remember in a traditional job you don't necessarily have the pleasure of pursuing your dreams freely because you have to work for the company's end game — *you* are their end game. Yet you remain disposable and could be let go at any time for any reason. Unless you're actively pursuing your dreams, someone has probably hired you to fulfill theirs.

I can maybe count on one hand the people who spoke life into me and said, "Go after everything you want and don't look back. You are talented, hungry, and more than capable. I believe in you!" Even if those comments were in a passing statement, those words had so much power that they dug in deep and began to grow in my thoughts until I started believing it. Words like that can be so rare, but are so powerful. The crazy part is that they were not a foreign concept when they said them. It actually confirmed what was already inside, but their declarations seemed to uncover them.

One of my favorite things to do is get in front of people and ask them what they could do, and would do, if they had enough time and money to wake up every day and paint their dreams on a blank canvas.

Did you go blank when you read that last statement? What would you do? There isn't a five-year-old on the planet who doesn't think they're going to be an astronaut, or a princess, or a super hero. It's in every thought, action, and even the games children play. Listen to what the little ones are saying next time you're near them. Imagine if you talked to yourself like they do? What could you be and do? You see, what the kids say is actually normal, what you have believed and say about yourself is NOT.

Being a kid in spirit is normal, and it's who you are, and it's still in there somewhere. What is abnormal is to shut out the thoughts because you have to be "realistic." You had to have dreaming beaten out of you by the world and by the multitudes who have settled, and they really want you to join them. Misery loves company, after all.

I hope that you decide to speak in somebody's life today, starting with your own. There is a world of people out there who need a phone call or an encouraging word. You don't know what's going on behind the scenes. There's a lot of people who are right on the edge and need a voice, even if it's just one voice to let them know they are not stuck, and their dreams are still within reach.

Think of the power of just reaching out and making a call.

For example, if I didn't get a phone call about our current opportunity because someone cared enough to share it wih me, we would not live the life we do now! Let that sink in. I would have kept pressing on as I always did. I would have had a breakthrough sooner or later, **YOU CAN BELIEVE THAT**, but **THAT** call did it for us in a very big way!

I really hope this resonates with you. I'm going to help you jackhammer the crust that has built up around your ability to dream, to hear, to believe, and to act so you can walk like a warrior with a sword in your hand knowing that success is not optional, it's **MANDATORY**!

7. HOW MUCH IS ENOUGH?

My favorite answer is:
Just a little bit more!

One of my favorite quick read books is 212° The Extra Degree, by Sam Parker and Mac Anderson. The book explains in detail what the extra degree can produce in physics, sports, and life in general.

At 211°, water is hot. But, at 212°, the steam and pressure from that extra degree in temperature could power a steam ship across the ocean, or launch jets from an aircraft carrier. It's the little things that make all the difference, the results may even blow your mind!

When it comes to building your business, some of you are thinking, *"I'll add 20 new consultants a month!"* I hear you, and that's great. But if the average person in your organization added just one more consultant and just one more customer a month, that is huge, especially as that builds through an organization for a while. We have to remember that the majority of people who join network marketing companies did so to add a little "lift" to their lives, like $500, $1000, or $2000-ish a month, and generally continue to work the job they currently have. If you are a rockstar in this industry, fantastic! I love that! But your income is made up of a multitude who will only be customers and those who want only that "lift." We must remember that and create an environment that makes their goal valuable too, and not just the superstars.

Some people will see someone in their organization go crazy and start building like wild fire. I've heard their uplines say, "Hey, you're under me in the organization and making more than me. Wait a minute. What are you doing?" When they see the results came from simply doing income-producing activities and sharing the product and business with people consistently, they are blown away... as though this is a secret revelation! Always remember, the last guy in can make more than the first guy in, if he shares and has an organization that shares with more people. Not magic. Just math.

Have you ever noticed how companies parade top earners and producers around like crowd-surfing Rockstars? Showing off highly successful people should and does encourage the rest of the team and company to shine, I get that, but all too often it creates envy, jealously, and excuses within the ranks. Don't be that person. Be the person who is empowered by seeing others' success. I promise, that's more fun than making excuses and seeing others results as competition.

8. ACTION IS NOT FOR THE END OF THE MONTH

The end of the month 48-hour panic is not how you want to act as a leader. Notice I said leader? You are! Whether you have one consultant or one customer, you are a leader. As a leader what you do duplicates — good or bad — and how you do anything is how you do everything. Last-minute people create last-minute organizations, and an end of month panic can potentially create all kinds of issues that could be avoided.

Nobody Has Joined Me Yet

What if you can't seem to get anyone to join you, whether you're just starting, or you actually have been in your opportunity for a while? One major key to growing is to turn off all the noise. Literally, turn it off. I suggest putting your dream board in front of your television. So, in

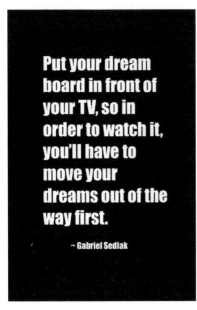

Put your dream board in front of your TV, so in order to watch it, you'll have to move your dreams out of the way first.

~ Gabriel Sedlak

order to watch TV, you'll have to move your dreams out of the way first.

How about urning off all the crazy notification on social media that have you reacting every time you hear a ding. Shut it off for 30 minutes to an hour so you can stay focused.

How many groups are you a part of on social media? Most of the time they're a distraction more than anything. They take you away from exposing your message to new people. Following the leader of the week, the personality of the month, and totally retooling the shop every month to accommodate all the new shiny information you're ingesting is just busy work. It may, on some level, motivate you because it feels like forward motion. But if it doesn't create income-producing activities, get rid of it. Turn off the noise.

People say you need a "why that makes you cry." In order to really start seeing things change. Haven't we all cried enough tears over the years? What really changed from the crying? Not too much!

I don't want to cry. I need a why that drives me to action. The why must go far deeper than making you cry. The kind of why that makes obstacles invisible! This is yet another reason I wrote this book. I want you to be so fed up, angry at the lack of results, and tired of being a spectator watching everyone else live, that you are compelled and driven to action until your breakthrough comes, because then it will!

9. GOALS YES, BUT DO YOU *SEE* THEM YET?

Sounds like a simple question, right? Let me give you a couple of examples. When my oldest son Ayden was 11, he read *Tales of the Odyssey*, about ancient Greek mythology. He shared with me a particular part in the story that hit him hard as he was reading, and his explanation was really instrumental in me writing this chapter. He said,

"Daddy, it's the most incredible thing. As I have been reading the Odyssey, I don't see words anymore. Everything I read I see and is being played out in my mind as though I'm standing in the middle of the adventure movie. So, I no longer read anymore. I pick up the book and immediately go on an adventure. It has changed the way I'll be reading anything from now on."

Wow is that a revelation! Honestly, it's a phenomenal place to be when your eyes and ears truly hear and see. When you see vision clearly, your surroundings disappear. You start living in such a profound place that you can actually revisit it whenever you choose. You're free of limitations and can actually win before you begin.

Another great example is a story I heard about about one of the first people to ever reach the peak of Mt. Everest. Reporters asked the man questions like,

What was it like when you were climbing up that first initial plateau?

When you crossed that ridge, did you want to stop, turn around, and go back?

Did the lack of feeling in your feet and hands make you think you may actually lose them?

What about the sudden snow storms and high winds? Did they surprise you and make you want to turn back?

Did you press forward in the storm or wait for that clear moment to climb the final part to the peak?

When you were finally there, what was it like to smell the air and see the curvature of the earth from that elevation?

And the gentleman said, "*It was actually just like every other time.*"

Do you understand what he said!? He had already been there in his mind! He already did it. The mechanics were just walking out what he saw played out hundreds of times before in his mind.

Before I ever actually brought my wife Holley home from

the mortgage industry, I was so hungry! I *saw* her coming down the spiral steps of her building and out the front door. I *saw* the look in her eyes, full of excitement and a bit of trembling, when I picked her up in our black Honda Odyssey minivan to leave her office for the last time! I *saw* us with our kids home-schooling, laughing, joking, and discovering as we traveled and experienced the world together, never missing a moment.

I *saw* it all. I could taste it. I could smell it. It was so clear to me that I don't even remember growing our business or any of the obstacles in the beginning when we launched it.

Everybody always asks me what I did to grow such a big organization? How did I talk to people the first year, when our opportunity literally was just launching? First, let me make it clear I didn't do it by myself. Yes, I was a vision caster, and I kept declaring hope and possibility until there was a

> **Obstacles do not exist when you love BIG enough.**
>
> ~ Gabriel Sedlak

breakthrough that became a movement. But is that by itself enough? No, the whole of the teams collective actions from all their hard work including mine, made our life possible. I have to make that clear especially in an industry where names and personalities are so often exalted. We all have a part to play to win the game. My actions alone could never have created that. To continue, Honestly, the first year was a *total* blur. All I remember is seeing my family together all the time, living life on our terms. So, walking out the mechanics was just as normal as breathing. Obstacles don't exist when you love big enough. When you're anchored on the vision, obstacles just simply have no power. They may be true, but they are not **the** truth. Building this business wasn't a labor. Like my son, I no longer read words. I was in my own story. I was reading and winning even before I actually walked in it. So declaring vision, hope, and possibility was easy! When you have a vision and a clarity like that, it becomes tangible and alive. When it's alive, it has feelings, emotions, and breath. That is how your "why" actually has power, because it's a living thing!

I love dream boards. People get really excited about having home gatherings and having "Dream Parties." They're super excited about making one and placing it in a prominent place in the home. I agree, and you need one badly! I have them myself, they're awesome, and if you don't have one yet, make it a priority. I'd love to have you share it with me some day!

The problem is, you can cut magazine clippings until you go cross-eyed. You can glue enough stuff to it to make every person in your neighborhood a dream board. Still, that alone will not create change. You need to see yourself in it like a movie running before your eyes, and guess who the star is in the movie? **YOU ARE!**

I don't mean just putting exciting things on a board to show yourself that you want this or that. I've done that. My question is: What's in your heart of hearts? It's like falling in love. When you find the one, you don't need sleep, food, or anything else for that matter. Your vision is consumed with a movie running every minute seeing the one you love. As you watch it, it's packed with scenarios, little and big adventures, special moments, smells, and tastes, saturating your emotions as you watch. Nothing like it on earth. **NOTHING!**

The things on your vision board with superficial fluff come and go. They're usually a passing fancy. You'll end up getting some of those things, but it's the real emotional and personal things that truly have the power to drive you.

You look up one day and suddenly you're surrounded by THOSE things on the dream board. I can attest to it. There has never been one thing that I genuinely connected with that I haven't received. Vision boards are serious business! Don't treat them as cute or lighthearted. I didn't say don't make it fun but treat it like it has nuclear power. Because it does! Really dig deep and allow yourself the grace of regularly changing your board as you begin the *see* things more and more clearly. Don't create another mental gymnastics event for yourself that just turns into another empty action. That doesn't produce anything. You have to taste it. You can't just see the words anymore. You need to *taste* the moment. You don't need to worry about the concerns of *how* to climb your Everest, because by going deep into this place, you will have already done it.

Talk about changing lives, this CAN DO IT! So many can be set free because of your example, it's crazy! *You cannot take people where you haven't been, and you cannot give what you don't have.* You cannot take concepts and relate their beauty to people. Only when you have had it in your hands can you share it.

Be militant about what you want and where you want to go. We've done it. We've lived it. We're *living* it. And we continue to constantly push ourselves to reach for impossibilities until we have them in our hands.

You are a CHAMPION!

You were born a CHAMPION!

And for those of you who have kids, they desperately need to see that CHAMPION, because something else will if you're not!

Victory is the best example you could ever give anyone. The people watching you are going to get caught up in the momentum you create all because you had a breakthrough!

10. AHHH, YES....
REJECTION

L et's talk about rejection. There is this very prevalent idea in our industry that seems to hang over everybody's head. It causes people to be extremely introspective, soft, apologetic, and sometimes just flat-out silent. They end up constantly fine-tuning and trying to tweak how they say stuff and how they posture themselves when sharing about their opportunity. In this section we will cut to the root so that rejection no longer presents itself as an issue.

The truth is that rejection is actually a myth. YES, I SAID IT — MYTH!

Let's say I own an ice cream shop. You come in and say, *"Hi there! I couldn't help but notice your shop. I sure do love ice cream! What flavors do you have?"*

And I say, "Hey! Thanks for coming in. You are going to love our ice cream. Today we have chocolate, vanilla, and strawberry, and I can even mix them for you if you want more than one flavor."

Then you take a pause and say, *"Hmmm. No thanks. I'm not really in the mood for any of those flavors, I was looking for something a bit more exciting, but thanks anyway."*

As the owner, do I get upset? Do I tuck my tail between my legs, walk into the back and cry? Do I think to myself, *"I don't even know why I started an ice cream shop? I hate selling. I hate rejection, and I hate the feeling when someone walks away! I am thinking about quitting!"*

You would never do that! You would just say, *"Hey, no problem. Maybe next time when you come in, we'll have something you like. Have a great day!"*

I want you to understand that most "rejection" is just a simple misalignment of a fit. When you go to buy a car, you go to the dealership and the salesperson explains each vehicle's specific features. You even drive a couple of different models, but you find there is not really anything that's grabbing you. Nothing fits your current needs and wants.

So, you say,

"Thanks so much. Let me get your card. I'm going to look around at a couple of other brands and see what they have. I'll let you know what I decide. Thanks so much for your time."

Does the salesperson say to his managers,

"Are you kidding me? We needed that sale! All the time I spent with those people, and they're going somewhere else! Statistics show if people leave the dealership and go to another

place, there is a high probability they will buy from them. Maybe the car business just doesn't work for me?"

Does the dealer say,

"I think we need to find another salesperson. John didn't follow the process or the closing technics. Those people would have bought if John did his job properly."

Come on, people! Of course not!

Okay, one more example!

Let's say that you're designing a deck on the back of your house. You have an idea of what you want, and you want it to tie into the pool and back grass area. You have a company doing a bid and they have agreed to draw up a few plans that you can look through. Hopefully you'll like one and you'll hire them to do the job. You look at what they've come up with and you're just not seeing it.

So, you say,

"I really appreciate what you came up with. I need to talk it over, see what other designs are out there, and I'll get back to you if we decide to move forward."

Does the designer freak out and say?

"Those are my best ideas. They are not going to find better plans anywhere else. They seriously need my ideas if they really want their house to look decent. I'm so sick and tired of spending all my precious time and then have people say they'll think about it. I'm not sure I'm cut out for the design business."

No! They are thinking about it. It may or may not be a fit. It is as simple as that. What about any of these examples has anything to do with rejection!?

Just like your products and opportunity, people don't always immediately jump in when you're sharing it with them. They do not always embrace everything you are saying wholeheartedly and are not always emotionally moved to the degree you are. Are you shocked when they don't join on the spot? If someone tells you they need to go home and think about it, do you take that fairly common answer as rejection? Hang on! You just got another "no," which means you're getting closer to a "yes." Right? Truthfully, I can't stand that logic and training! It's actually wiring you improperly. Only the people who see other people as numbers can function in such a strange state of mind. No matter how clever it sounds, I can tell you that this kind of glass-half-empty logic will hurt you far more than help you.

Thinking like this creates a *predetermined mission*. Remember we talked about "seeing" things and that you need to have faith in what you have expectations for? Going for "no" subconsciously, and then consciously, becomes what you work toward. It's no wonder so many fail by thinking they can be successful using the "numbers game" and "go for no" logic when trying to build their business. The most tragic part about all this logic is that it dehumanizes the person you're speaking with. You reduce your business to simply filling the spaces with names. Your business is nothing if people aren't valued and listened to above everything else. They are alive with passions and fears and have to be given respect, even if they say no.

If it's not a fit, it's not a fit. It may happen later, but it has nothing to do with rejection. People don't always remember what you said, but they do remember how they felt when they were with you. How they felt when they left you may determine if they ever come back to you again.

I can hear it now! Some of you are saying, "Ah! So then going for YES is the key!" Whoa, not so fast! We are going to go a little deeper, yet the answer is so obvious it's nuts! Working for "yes" is light years better across the board than working for "no," but that's not the answer either. Let me share something so simple that it virtually removes all of the mess and the many rabbit trails that are weaved all over and through our industry.

Of course, you will tailor the following to your company and products....

"Thanks for sitting down and chatting for a few to hear more about the products and opportunity. Like I did, I'm sure you'll see yourself fitting in somewhere. But, before I go into more detail, let me share briefly why I said yes and joined."

I said this near the beginning of the book, and here it is again...

* *T*ell your brief story and journey.

* Then a brief history of the company. If you have a video or PowerPoint, use then I suggest using that to share the message. Why reinvent the wheel?

* Then ask how they see themselves fitting in.

WARNING: Don't try to be the expert! Be an expert at sharing your story and be the expert at using the company's resources instead!

Rejection is a myth. If it's not a fit, it's not a fit. If someone wants to be a customer, perfect. If they want to be a consultant, perfect. If someone wants to be a runner, perfect. If someone has no interest but will refer you to the right people, perfect!

If it's not a fit, how on earth is that rejection? Your job is to share your story and the different parts of the opportunity and allow people to fit where they see themselves. Over time people will surprise you. They do not generally stay only in one category. I have had people say no to all of it in the beginning then ended up saying yes and went on to build huge businesses. I have had customers only who then became powerhouse consultants. I have seen consultants who ended up only becoming a customer after they said they were going to change the world. I have seen people leave to do other things. I have had people drop off the earth with no reason why. I have had people join, tiptoeing in the beginning, then someone in their team explodes and that momentum is what ends up setting them on fire, and that is when they started really running with their business.

Not all cars fit all people, Not all clothes fit all body types and tastes. Not all homes are a fit for every family. Not everybody can be in the same career, and not everybody can or will be in your opportunity. Your job is to share and let them decide whether it's a fit or not. We are looking for the people who are looking for us, and that is perfect!

11. THIS INDUSTRY IS A GIFT

F ind me a traditional companies that will fight for you and support your goals and dreams, who does that? Not many.

I say, at the very least, treat your home-based business with half of the intensity and faithfulness you do with your current job, that likely sees you as disposable.

We can give 110% to a company, never take a sick day, miss all kinds of important events and moments with our family for years, and yet there could be a box on your desk after twenty years of doing everything right. Over the years, I've had very emotional conversations with countless executives and every other level of business person. They've sat in front of me and said, "I don't even understand your industry or your business model. You share a story and drink coffee? I went to school for

> At the very least, treat your home based business with half of the intensity and faithfulness you do with your current job that likely sees you as a disposable.

twelve years plus many more years of college after that. I have a degree, and all you do is drink coffee and share?"

Obviously, I do more than that, but if you really whittle down the essence of the business, it is really that simple and is what has given us the most success. So, yes, that is what I do.

I love to hear all the crazy things people actually think we do that created our success. I actually like asking people what they think we did that made us have the success we have. As funny as some of the answers are, as we talk more, of course I demystify so many of the assumptions and the rhetoric that's out there. People just say what they say, and believe what they believe, usually because of ignorance about our industry, or they haven't tasted what a good opportunity can actually do when ther right mindset is attached to it. Maybe they saw someone else in network marketing fail, act weird, or exhibit some "cult-like" behavior. Maybe they just flat-out really didn't know what else to say.

Think about this:

I decide that I want a parrot. I'm super excited because I've done my research, and I figured out the exact type of parrot I want. I go to the closest exotic pet store because I find out they are the best pet stores to get that kind of parrot. As soon as I walk in the door, I see this beautiful parrot sitting there perched by the door. It was almost like he was smiling at me. Yup, that's the one I want. I quickly let an employee know I want to take him home. She told me all the things he can do, how smart the birds are, and that they are really great at repeating everything they hear. And after getting comfortable in his new surroundings when I get him home, he should start having little conversations with me.

That has me and my kids super excited! I get him home and all settled in a perfect place by the big window so he can see outside. He is quiet for a few days because of the transition, which was expected. Then one night I'm startled out of sleep because I hear dogs barking in the house. I think it's a dream, but then it continues. I get up, turn all the lights on, thinking it may be one of my neighbors' dogs. I walk in to see if the parrot is okay. He is just staring at me bug eyed, so I turn off the lights and go back to bed. This happens several nights in a row, so I finally have enough! I decide to sit in the living room with a flashlight and wait for just that time when I start hearing dogs barking. So, guess what happens? Yep you guessed it! Lo and behold, the parrot begins to bark and bark loud! So, I call the pet store when they open and ask them what's going on. After asking several people that know the bird's history, I learn that the parrot was raised next to the dog kennels when he was small before he came to the pet store. Isn't that interesting! I buy this exotic bird, do all my research, and yet when I bring him home, he barks like a dog! And THAT, my friends, is exactly what people are like!

Most of the world was raised next to dogs, and they

bark. When talking about network marketing or entre-preneurship in general, many people just repeat what they've heard and have been exposed to.

A few years back in a large training session I was doing, I gave some kickback to somebody. I don't necessarily suggest it, but it was just one of those times. The husband of one of our consultants showed up to add pressure on his wife because he did not approve of her new business. He asked me in that open setting, I'm sure to embarrass her, "Hey, so you really seem to be the guru in this company. You are the one my wife has been talking about. Are you kidding me? I would never do what you do. Isn't this one of those things that you have to sell stuff and you are the guy at the top making all the money and everyone's sales and work basically fills your pockets, right? I have a degree. Sounds like a pyramid scheme to me."

I knew this was a moment I couldn't resist, so I paused for an uncomfortable period of time just to make my point. Terrible, I know. I've matured a bit since then. I asked him what he did for a living. After he told me the company he worked for, I asked him if he was a valuable employee, how long he worked there, how many hours a week he was away from home. He proudly proclaimed 60+ hours a week, and I asked if he made the company better and more profitable for working there. He proudly said, "Yes!" I said, "Are you kidding me? Is that one of those jobs where you have to sell stuff to keep your job and you have to be away from your family and work 60+ hours a week, missing games, driving in traffic, and getting paid just enough to keep you there, but not enough to allow you to leave? Do you have to keep your job for your benefits, even though they could let you go at any time? I would never do one of those pyramids."

Boy did he glare at me! I continued.

"Come on, man," I said, *"You have chosen your career based on the information you were given and made the best choice possible for your family, right? Well, based on the information I had, and the lives I saw people living because of network marketing, I made the decision to do what I do because of the freedom it gives me and my family, both in time and money. The best part is we never have to miss a moment. We should talk more so you can really understand what this business is about. Your wife is really doing great, and I think you'd be pleasantly surprised."* He never took me up on my offer.

People are conditioned to bark. They say stuff based upon filters, ignorance, information, and misinformation. I do not spend much time trying to educate the people who dig their heels in with opinions. It's exhausting, and they rarely end up joining anyway. I simply share the story and if they don't go my direction, that's great. If they join me, fantastic. My job is not to try to persuade the world to do what I do. My job is to find those who are willing and are looking for something more.

Another time, in an even larger meeting, a very successful businessman got a bit aggressive with me about what I was sharing. He stood up and said to the whole room that I insulted his intelligence and the years he poured into his degrees.

He said that because I mentioned designing my life on purpose to never miss a moment, never finished high school, and that I really failed all the way through school, but eventually got a GED in my 20s, this man felt that it just couldn't really be the whole story. He said the clincher was when I said that all you need is passion, fire, and hunger in your belly to change anything. And because I said that if I were to give my resume to an employer, all it would include is three big words in crayon and my name at the top. That *really* got him upset.

Please note that my intention in sharing my story the way I did was to let the room know that I was the least qualified person in the room, and if I could do it, I was sure they could too.

Resume skills:
1. Passion
2. Fire
3. Hunger
~ Gabriel Sedlak

People could see that this man was a little heated with quite an intense tone when he started talking.

WARNING: There's always one in every meeting! In life, your critics will do more to promote you than your fans ever will by the way.

After listening to his points, I said,

"Sir, I'm sorry if you're bothered by what I said. You should rejoice with me that somebody like me, with my background and lack of 'education' can have a chance to do big things in life because of the power of network marketing. If I can live the life I do because of the power of this industry to create leverage, which creates financial and time freedom. Imagine

someone like yourself who blows me away in every area, espe-cially job experience and education. Imagine what you could accomplish!"

Can you tell I matured a bit by that point from the prior example? Thank goodness!

He froze, stared at me for a while, and said, *"Let's talk after the meeting."* So afterward he walked up to me and said,

"I was thinking more about how you responded to me, and, man, you're right! When I came at you like I did, you just re-sponded with truth. You just hit every area in my life talking tonight, and it made me angry. I gave up so much, and I was one of those you were talking about who did listen to all the opinions out there. Those opinions steered me away from my dreams for years, even though I made a ton of money. See, you simply said yes, and didn't have to go the path I did, and that really ticked me off. Do you have some time this week to chat over coffee?"

Now that was a good meeting, and we both learned a lot. He went away with a greater respect for me and our industry.

You see, leverage is what creates every wealth model. Either you have it, or you're being leveraged. You can change the world if you will champion that message alone! People really need to hear it, whether you get kickback or not.

People believe, "hard" money is good money, but "easy" or easier money is bad money. Wrong! Leverage doesn't care if you are used by it or you are using it to its maximum level. The question is, what side of it are you on? Leverage and/or residual income must be in play if you're going to see freedom and have a beach-money lifestyle.

> If someone's opinion has the power to take you off course, just make sure they are willing to pay your bills 10 years from today, because you may have just allowed them to steal your future.
> ~ Gabriel Sedlak

If someone's opinion has the power to take you off course, just make sure they are willing to pay your bills ten years from today because you may have just allowed them to steal your future. Do you know what's worse than others' opinions? You allowing it by putting stock in their words over your own.

Perfect example. My mom was told she would never be a good driver and couldn't drive. Family members and the people who filled a position of value to her cemented this belief in her heart when they said it.

When my mother was told that she could never drive, she was already emotionally depleted and overwhelmed. So, believing statements, instead of rejecting them, was not very hard. She had no emotional defenses up by that point. Rather than having the power to say NO WAY, I will not be a victim, she saw herself unable to drive. Fear took over and paralyzed her from action. We had two perfectly functional cars on two different occasions sitting in our driveway. As the months rolled on and became years, they sat there and sat there. Occasionally a friend would come by and jump start them and drive them up the road and back, then put them back where they were parked before. I actually used them as play toys, pretending to drive them, and used them as a fort. Because of words, we spent $600 to $800 a month in the 1970s on taxi fare! The taxis would pull up the driveway and honk for us to come out as we walked right past the cars and crawled in the taxi. As a kid, that was a hard one to understand. We paid somebody else to take us around because of beliefs.

People are stuck at every level imaginable. From the down and outers to the up and outers. Even the perfect couple in the suburbs with the big house, nice clothes, and expensive cars, from the outside, they look like they have it all together. Often, these people are more stuck and miserable than you would ever be allowed to see. The nice things just work as an excellent shield to hide what's going on behind the scenes. Do I think that network marketing can fix all the challenges life tries to throw on us? No, of course not. But if there is a business model that has the power to give us time back and the ability to hope again, isn't it worth changing our mindsets and going after it? If people understood the power of our industry, they would line up down the street in front of your house just to have that conversation.

12. THE BIG ONES

D o not read through this next section fast, as a matter of fact you may just decide to skip it all together. I even considered not putting it in the book, but it is so important, that my conscience wouldn't allow me to not. Reading it, really reading it, may take a a hour, a day, or a week, but I promise you, it controls far more than you may have ever imagined, so don't rush through this.

Time to step on some very popular pet beliefs that have marinated the minds of people all through the ages. People *must* attempt to make sense of what they are going through. You certainly don't have to believe like I do, and I may loose some of you for good after this, and that's OK. But I can attest to the fact, that my family and I have experienced the beauty, wonder, and freedom of getting untangled from the following:

1) "I just believe ALL things happen for a reason."

What reason? Does that mean *whatever* the outcome is.....

then THAT outcome is THE answer to the reason? All things, like everything? Statements like this are said so often in passing by people you would think it's an exact scientific fact of life.

Actually, there is a reason all things happen. Big difference! You can always trace back the series of events that caused a particular thing to occur. People are desperate to explain their current experiences and almost always point to an outside controlling force. Let me make clear one important part of this. I am very aware that God truly orchestrates things to create a beautiful end or for our divine protection. I have had, and still have, both happen regularly in my life. My wife and I have an incredible testimony that we can't wait share more about in a future book, and plan for it to be on video as well, so we can go into detail about how God moved heaven and earth to put us together. We are living proof of His goodness!

Yet when people say *ALL* things happen for a reason (I'm dealing with the word *all* here) Whether destructive, evil, positive, delays, non answers, sickness, healing, health, lack of health, things working out, things not working out, business growth, lack of business growth, people joining you, people not joining you, terrible relationships, or loosing a job. The list is endless. They end up being all bunched up in one big pile, and almost always are attributed to God as the author. That's a problem. This position assumes you aren't in control *at all*, and are not responsible *at all,* so coasting and letting the wind blow you to *whereverland* was all meant to happen, wherever that is. It's not a cosmic soup controlling you, surprising you every time you dip your spoon in it.

Good is not evil and evil is not good, positive is not negative and negative is not positive. Even calling it "neutral equal forces", or to say that they really aren't inherently good, evil, positive, or negative, and that they are just labels we put on them, and it is actually all part of the cosmic recipe, is also wrong.

The concept that God *creates* or *allows* an evil or negative event to happen, to then use that same event to jump in and boldly *save the day* is also a gross misunderstanding of who He is. There are not two sides of that same coin. We're not talking Greek mythology here, where Zeus and Hades are brothers, and both love and hate each other at the same time, where mankind reaps all the ills from their cosmic chess match. To make it more plain for a moment, from a theological side, the devil is NOT the opposite of God....if you want to use that argument then he would be a stripped and powerless opposite version of Michael the archangel. **BIG, MASSIVE DIFFERENCE!**

It's not a "force" where light and darkness each work together holding hands to create just the perfect amount of tension that keeps all things in balance in the universe. I say universe, because it's a super popular blanket term used by many these days to explain anything that happens, or will happen.

If all these positions are attributed to God, then He is the most schizophrenic being ever, and he constantly destroys what he creates, and if that were true, then we all really have far bigger problems! Getting this stuff straight is critical, whether you think of yourself *"religous"* or not. Because these concepts are so deeply baked into the cookie, people are still influenced from them at a grand scale, whether they can identify the ingredients as they take a bite on not, it is still being ingested into their thinking. Not understanding this will cause you to embrace things, thinking that He has a *plan* for putting "*it*" on you. Because of that, you won't reject lies or contrary circumstances, you won't cast them away and take authority over them. Instead you will embrace them in neutrality and simple wait for whatever result(s) that comes, believing it was *meant to happen*.

Yes, life does come at us, and yes it does bring with it all kinds of challenges, but we must be able to discern the source and the difference, so we won't embrace what we should be rejecting, and reject what we should be embracing.

YES, God can and does **NEVERTHELESS** make all things work out for those that trust him. He is willing and able to make the original negative situation not even have the smell of smoke once he's redeemed it. But to attribute Him as the souce of the original problem is perverse.

2) "If it's meant to happen then it will all work out."

This is the cousin of the first one, and very similar in it's beguilement. It will be close to the first one in explanation, but ever so slightly different.

Who's actually in charge of it *working out?* You can't use something not working out, to assume that someone or something stopped it. Or it working out to assume it was the will of the one who orchestrated it to work out. The word *"meant"* is personal and has intent, and if it's personal, then something or someone purposed it. Then you have a whole new set of questions. Who was it? Why was it done? Why do they care to see it happen to me? Are you helpless and powerless to change it? Or do you believe that you are not supposed to ask or know, just blindly trust. People always use hindsight to justify and make sense of current circumstances, and use it *working out* to *their* favor as being *ordained*. So if the end result is what they want, or they can make logical sense of, or be OK with the result, then, it was *meant* to happen. This one is commonly used to excuse things not working out rather than making it work out, or rerouting the approach when there are setbacks, or evaluating why it didn't work out, and re-strategizing to make it work out! Whatever happens was meant to be, as we are blown around by whatever wind blows, because all of it was *meant to happen.*

3) "That was meant to happen so you can help people who have been through similar circumstances."

This is the other cousin....

No! It happened. *Nevertheless,* is a word you have to get your head around. Yes, those things that happened, and can be used as a positive learning experience that can always be used to benefit future situations or to help people in similar circumstances. By all means, use your experience to help people, we all do that all the time, it's natural. And yes, God can take something that happened (meaning something negative) and turn it around, but to use the word *"meant"* again assumes something or someone controlled, intended or allowed a situation. These examples again almost always have God as the author, regardless of the outcome. If you reach in the grab bag and get a cookie, then God allowed you to grab it for a snack. If you reach in the bag and grab a scorpion, and it stings you, then God allowed it to sting you to teach you a lesson. Now you'll be able to share with others what it was like to have a scorpion sting you. He allowed it so you can help people who have been or will be stung by scorpions.

If, no matter what you do, what is *meant* to happen is ultimately going to happen, then why pray, why try, why do anything? Now lace that in *religious talk* and people become paralyzed and are forced to accept the *grab bag of life* results. God is painted with a mysterious and unknowable persona, and you don't know if you're going to be slapped or hugged. He's painted as *mysterious* and all you can do is *hope and pray,* never really knowing what the answer will be, and that's a horrible way to hope and believe.

Hope must be anchored on knowing what you are putting your hope in, or the nature, personality, and ways, of the author of hope. Praying should be a confident action, not blind, and not begging.

Petitioning someone you know confidently, allows you to request according to their nature, will, and ability, and because you know them, and they gave you their word, THE Word, you can then confidently pray. Prayer is not supposed to be an empty, check the box, religious action, it is powerful, and there is a real reason for it. Praying with that clear, exact, and measured intent, allows you to properly and accurately, (based on that *knowing*) agree in prayer to see it enforced or manifested. You are confident that God is able and willing to answer, and not answer in some *mysterious gumbo-like nebulous* manner. Religious ideology is *always* the problem. Even Jesus himself rebuked the religious people for making life far more difficult than it was, and for clouding up Gods true nature, which derails people and forces additional rules and laws, which causes judgment and fear. We are taught to trust and never question this *unknown* and accept *whatever* results are handed to us.

There are not enough lifetimes to go through all the stuff that was *meant* to make you qualified enough to help enough people going through all the millions of possible scenarios in life. I hope what I just said sets your mind free. I know it's a bit heavy, but I have never seen more people paralyzed by fear, indecision, and the *"whatever's meant to be will be"* rhetoric. When you know your Father and how good He is, and the power we have been given, and you understand His nature and His love, you'll never again think a slap is a hug.

I hear this rhetoric daily, as I'm sure you have. Maybe you are the one saying it? Well-meaning ideas, said by good people that sound good, can become ingrained beliefs that are held on to when situations in life are vague or not clearly understood. Most of the time they become the blanket answer for whatever happens. We went through the Dark Ages not by accident, but because for over 1000 years light and truth was stripped away and removed from the masses across the world by relegious and controlling leaders. And where truth and light are absent, all kinds of *replacements* show up to fill it.

Unchecked, you won't use your God-given authority,

and you won't take the tools given to you to change things and fight. Instead, you become a puppet with your strings pulled in every direction, powerless to resist, and are a victim of the wind however it may blow.

13. EVERYTHING YOU DO MATTERS TO EVERYONE, ALWAYS

E verything that I say, everything you say, and everything that is said to people creates a chain reaction. Sometimes the smallest little nugget becomes the trajectory for somebody's complete and total life change. This whole thing is a battle between the ears. It always amazes me that the thought life and what you "see" is the place where conception occurs. When something is conceived, it has everything in it already to bloom to full maturity. And if it's in an environment to grow safely, what happens? Not only is it alive, but eventually it's able to function all by itself. Our children should be illustration enough here.

How about the past, especially the negative past? You have a sudden thought. It comes externally, seemingly from out of nowhere, but ends up festering. You can't seem to shake it off, and the imagery begins to get more and more vivid, to the point it becomes like it's actually happening again. Then it's played out into kind of a mini movie. You begin to replay and actually feel those ugly feelings and emotions. They begin to become alive in your members. After a while, they become so real that you're back where you were. This is one big reason why people can't get over the past, and past failures, because they recreate it over and over again into their present. (You may want to read the Frankenstein section in the beginning of the book again)

Acting on thoughts doesn't happen immediately. Do we really think unfaithfulness starts with the act? No. It's a mental game that is allowed to fester in the imagination until it's already happened so vividly that acting on it is easy. How about theft? It's a planned-out process that is then acted on after the mental scenario is played out. Why do you think in the courtroom the sentencing for pre-meditated murder is so strong? It's because it wasn't an accident.

If the ugliness of life can be created or repeated this way, through thoughts and words, what could happen when this power is understood in a righteous, life giving, or godly way? The action is simply a byproduct of what had been conceived with thoughts. That is why the scripture says you have to take every thought captive.

You can choose to start your day however you want.

My wife and I start every day with a pot of coffee early in the morning in quiet. We talk, listen to a teaching, dream, and edify each other in our conversation before we allow the day to present itself to us. Even our kids know not to come downstairs until we have had our time first, usually an hour, many times two. I believe you need to start your day *seeing* something until you are walking in it. I suggest putting what you *see* on your dream board and meditate on it until you are already there. We do!

Old Fashioned House Cleaning

One of the keys to preparing the ground so your resolve and vision remain is to do a good old-fashioned "house cleaning." So many times we plead and pray for change, read all the books, go to all the classes, and declare all the right things. The problem is that we cocoon ourselves with the same unhealthy stuff. We still listen to the same voices. We still watch the same junk. We still refuse to get rid of those items with memories attached to them, especially from an unhealthy past relationships or experiences. We still listen to the same opinions from the same people who haven't changed in years and have the same drama. We hang out with the same defeated people who won't help you get better, I can promise you that!

There is a constant war between the vision you see in

your head and what seems like the reality around you. You're constantly trying to get motivated, but nothing in life changes. That's because both sides are being fed and are being built simultaneously, causing a cancelling out of each side. What you feed always wins. But if you starve one, then victory for the other is easy!

You must be militant and merciless against contrary voices, circumstances, and the familiar that keeps you in neutral! You need to force an awakening that exposes any affection or affinity for the things that controlled you. It's only painful because it has rooted itself into your personality so you actually believe it's you. The familiarity deceives you into drinking from it on a regular basis to maintain a neurotic state of unhealthy comfort.

See yourself free in super vivid detail, regardless of what anybody else is saying, or the results you may have gotten in the past. That, my friend, is how *you* gain ground. My family's future was at stake, and **THAT** hit me like a ton of bricks! I suddenly no longer cared for the familiar because I finally saw it for what it was.

Do you understand that most people won't even participate in their own deliverance?

I want you to conceive something that is so magnificent and so much larger than where you are now that it feels impossible. Because if it doesn't feel impossible, it's not big enough. If you can conceive it in your head and put it together in ten minutes, then stop! IT'S NOT BIG

ENOUGH! It must be something that makes you uncomfortable believing in it. It needs to embarrass you. Are you embarrassed to share that level of vision for your life with others?

If the answer is yes, congratulations! You're beginning to step into a proper way to live.

14. MEEKNESS

What do you think of when you read the word meekness? One of the most ancient and earliest definitions of meekness was presented to me by a friend about twenty years ago. I was at a really tough point in my life due to some external situations that I allowed to eat at me. I was at my apartment where I lived alone, and I hadn't left for about two weeks. My friend knocked at the door and told me he'd been thinking and praying for me, and he had no idea why, he just felt he should come over, and he didn't know I was shut up in my apartment either. He said he was going on a day trip to New Orleans, and if I didn't have anything better to do, I should join him. I agreed. After we drove for a while, my friend said, "Do you know what meekness means?" I answered, "I would love to say I did, but at this point I'm not sure I know what much of anything means." He said, "Great! When I was praying for you, I just knew this was for you today." Then he continued to explain.

One of the most powerful and ancient original meanings of the word "meek" comes from properly "meeking" horses before they were given as gifts to kings or great leaders in the ancient world. Many times the horses were given very young so the training process could happen as the horse grew and the leaders connected with the horse right along side the growth. A meeked horse was one of the greatest gifts you could give rulers because a meeked horse would respond to the rider as if they had one mind. In a dangerous situations, that horse and rider would live to see another day. Young horses were trained to listen to sounds, gestures, and input from the voice and breath of the rider so that when the rider had an inkling the horse would respond. If your horse had an instinct to move, the rider would sense it and follow, and vice versa. A true one-minded partnership. The horses were trained to not be spooked or sidetracked by noise, yelling, swords, other horses, the clamor of battle, or even if the horse was struck. Anything that could distract the horse, create a dangerous response, or create fear was worked out of it until the now grown horse was basically numb to anything but the voice and breath of the rider. That horse could face the horizon, any circumstance, and be pointed to plow through with such intensity that it was like a tank mowing over everything in its path.

I told my friend that I have struggled with the feelings of lying down. I felt that being meek was some kind of weird humility that I had to do, to embrace no matter what was happening to me. I felt like pushing through when I saw a door closed or the wall up was improper, ungodly, even wrong. I felt paralyzed to do anything. I believed if the door is closed, then I shouldn't push on it. I should simply wait for another to open. If one didn't open, then that's what was "meant" to be.

I looked at my friend and told him I don't think I will

look at my life the same again after today. He said, "See, I was supposed to come to your house today."

To train yourself to pay zero attention to contrary circumstances, you must cultivate the environment that will create a good ground for your seeds to grow. You must keep the foxes out of your fields and the crows off your corn! If you do, you can see real change and quickly! Don't be surprised if a whole new group of friends replaces your old ones, and don't be surprised if you are misunderstood for a time. Your victory will be an example that some will follow and be forever changed because you realized your worth. The people who choose to turn off the noise and press on until they reach green un-trampled fields will end up living a champion life. No power on earth is stronger than your ability to choose.

I know it feels good to be validated by people we know and are in the habit of listening to. Don't fall prey to that. Some things are too important to declare prematurely. Let the world see all your green fields and full harvest. Get to the point where no one can question it. Some will be jealous and try to take it from you, but they ultimately must go through this same process themselves to get it. Put yourself in an environment where you're celebrated — not tolerated — and don't leave! That atmosphere will add value and power beyond measure. The new friendships you make will make you wonder if you ever even had friends at all before.

When we got started in our current company, we had unity and vision and declared it until people joined the cause and desired the same. That created more unity. A few people gathered, then a few more people gathered, then many gathered, all because we created culture, hope, and vision. We were vision casters. To create a culture, you have to create a community around a common cause.

Can you imagine yourself successful and are you okay with it? You really need to be. It's not wrong to have success and to have things. But don't change your heart. Take all of your stuff away and who are you? You better be the same person with everything and the same person with nothing. Remember money only makes you more of who you are. If you're a benevolent, giving, empowering, and loving person, you'll be doing a lot more of it. If you're controlling, power hungry, selfish, manipulative, gossipy or perverse, you'll just do it a lot more.

One of the reasons network marketing is so incredibly valuable is because it can offer so much to the people who go for it. Not too many other things out there can do that for the average person. It's *impossible* to be successful in network marketing unless you have helped to change many lives. Success and serving others to be successful are inseparable! If you can see yourself successful one day, then when you get there, you won't be on the stage alone.

15. THE OBVIOUS IS OFTEN MISSED

I want to give a very basic and fundamental fact. The more sales there are, the more money there is. Shocking, huh? You could be the most prepared, the most knowledgeable, and the most trained consultant in your company. You could know what your founders eat for breakfast every third Thursday, and it's not going to matter if you're not doing income-producing activities. That means creating a continuous inflow of product customers and consistently sharing the company story and business opportunity to new prospective business partners.

Knowing this and agreeing with me doesn't mean it will be done. I hear it all the time from people who are so weighted down from endless trainings, seminars, and books (And I love all this things!) *But more information without action will create massive frustration!* They are preparing to prepare, and getting ready to get ready. They know all of the products ingredients in extreme detail, all the science, all the data, all the statistics. Yet their checks are *not* growing! They never miss a meeting, follow the top people in their company and in this industry like hawks, know how to explain the latest incentive, and are probably better trained than the top folks. Still, their checks are *not* growing! You can know absolutely everything about everything and be the most prepared, knowledgeable, *broke* consultant in your company.

When it comes to building your business, it's great to know everything and you should know those things. But people are successful in network marketing because of how they think, and what they do, then duplicating that through the organization. When asked about their extreme success, I heard a couple say one time,

> *"We just love each other, love sharing the products, love sharing the opportunity, and we told everyone faithfully until we didn't even recognize our lives anymore!"*

Do you still think you need my best 45-second elevator pitch? The truth is that the people you meet for a brief moment don't want an elevator pitch. People want a human being who cares. One of the reasons many people who join an opportunity fall out and quit in this industry, is that they never really understood properly what they were joining and the hard work it was going to require to be successful. They didn't have the mindset yet, and *that* would have been discovered in the beginning if more care and questions were asked by the consultant signing them up. They probably should have just been customers, without the business side there to pressure them prematurely, and in time they may have warmed up to the idea of joining. It would be like lifting 300 pounds at the gym the first day, when starting with 75 pounds would have been best, but instead the 300 injured them and they never came back.

They really were only looking for and needed great products, and that is why they said yes in the first place. On the flip side, many customers never had the chance to properly hear the power and potential of the opportunity. The business side was never shared with them, or more often, it was done sheepishly which imprinted no real vision for what was possible, so the business was dismissed altogether.

16. OH, I'VE GOT FRIENDS WHO DO THAT

Wrong perception can keep opportunity from you.

T he idea that people may have heard of your opportunity, or maybe know someone who does it, causes many to believe that saturation has already happened. People wonder how they can grow a business when the perception is that so many are already involved. The truth is that most who have "heard" about the business still have no idea what the company is really about. Blanket statements like, "Everybody in my neighborhood sells it," (which is *not* true) create an immediate mental paralysis.

Please hear this: **Saturation is a myth!** Everyone in your neighborhood? Come on! Even if it were true, let's think beyond the neighborhood for a minute. How about your county, your city, your state, the country, the world? We must look past the end of our nose. There is a big world beyond it!

I love this one too: I've "exhausted" all my friends on social media. Really? How many friends do you have, and how many people are on social media? We are constantly putting limitations on ourselves, based upon illusions that we've somehow chosen to believe. These illusions are killing people's dreams in countless numbers on a daily basis. People actually think that the very limited perspective they have is an accurate snapshot of the world at large. **IT IS NOT!**

Did you know that millions of refrigerators are sold every year in the U.S., and yet almost everyone has one? Some people even have two.

How about cell phones? There are around 9 billion mobile connections worldwide. That's more than the world's population! And yet, every day countless new phones are sold all over the earth. People replace models and brands all the time. Do you think the phone industry has any intention of shutting its doors? Never! People are constantly cycling through various stages of a buying journey.

How about underwear? Have you seen how many new underwear companies have popped up lately offering a "better experience," even though everyone already has lots of underwear? The underwear business is booming! It seems like every product category is being reinvented lately. How does this happen? It starts with people with vision who are shameless about sharing that vision. Then they create awareness and simply build something better!

Someone may have told you "no" 90 days ago, but as life ebbs and flows and circumstance change, suddenly 90 days later they are now saying "yes." People are constantly turning 18 years old and can begin their own home-based business. People are constantly looking for great products that actually work. People are always changing jobs and looking for opportunity. People are constantly retiring and need more so they can live better as the years progress. Many people want to leave a legacy for their kids, but have no possible way to do it with the path they are on.

The groups you can count on in the coming years to grab onto network marketing are those entering the workforce, those who can't afford to exit the workforce, those who have retired from the workforce, and everyone in between!....Did you get that? In other words.....

E V E R Y O N E.

Don't allow yourself, your business, and the gift of opportunity you share to be snared by the false idea of saturation. It's a myth. Now go share your products and opportunity with the world! There are always more people to talk to, and there always will be.

17. ARE YOU REPELLING PEOPLE?

Some people are just scattered and all over the place, it's really hard for people to join that.

"*H*ey guys, I'm running a bit late. So sorry! The kids went nuts, and the babysitter was late, the dog had an accident on the floor, I had a friend call with an emergency, then I lost my keys, then I spilled a 40oz. drink from Sonic in my car, then there was a wreck on the freeway, and I couldn't find your number, sorry about that, I'll see you in 15 minutes."

Sound familiar? Have you been that person? Have you had it happen to you? Normal, understandable, no problem. Such is life. Now, in this all-too-common scenario, what happens next makes you question everything before you've even heard anything. Let's say that same person walks in the door after fumbling in their car for a few minutes, after already showing up to the coffee shop late. When they emerge they have their arms loaded with stuff. What stuff? Presentation material! They walk in the door of the coffee shop breathing hard and sweating. They look like they were just shot out of a cannon. They have a giant shoulder bag full of products, a computer bag, and another box. After about 5 minutes setting up everything, they give everyone a big sigh, and says, "Ahh, okay. You ready? Thanks for your patience!"

Stop! Can you imagine it? Extreme example...Maybe? But how many of you know people that are just frazzled, scattered, and all over the place?

What are you already thinking to yourself? Man, if I have to do all this, there is *no way* I'm going to lug all that around trying to sell this thing! Agreed! I'd feel the same way.

What you didn't see is that their company really is incredible, has amazing products, and has a very simple way to share it, including a PowerPoint presentation you can easily show on an iPad, **but the messenger can mess up the message!**

Here's my point. What you do duplicates, good or bad, easy or hard. So many people make it so hard on themselves by over-complicating things, and this makes it hard for others to join you. When they see you struggling with your bags and boxes, they don't want to put themselves in that situation.

When I meet people, I just walk in, grab a coffee with my iPad and ask what intrigued them to meet me and hear about my products and opportunity. Then I let them talk. This takes all the crazy away, and anyone can do that. **When anyone *can* do it, many *will* do it.**

Your opportunity could be offering free gold bricks to people out of the trunk of your car when they join, but they won't follow you across the street to get it if you make it hard. If you're not simple, if you're not caring and confident, and if you're not asking them about themselves, the whole thing begins to have holes in it from the start. Even if they join you, it may not last. It's not about you; it's about them.

That's why I make it easy — on myself and on the person I'm sharing it with. I carry nothing with me except my iPad with our presentation and a cup of coffee. I don't go into the conversation carrying a pile of stuff. Do I have products, of course I do, everything is about the products, but most of the time unless they ask for it beforehand I leave them in the car initially, so as not to overwhelm *them*! If and when the conversation comes to them wanting to touch and feel the products, and the digital catalog wasn't enough, then I'll go grab a few things. Following this laid-back way of doing business will make people feel incredibly comfortable with you, and they'll be able to envision themselves doing the same thing! I always relax and tailor every meeting to be about them. If I am presenting the products and opportunity through video chats, one on one, or a large group online, I *still* keep it very easy and uncluttered.

I'm The Kind Of Person Who...

"Gabriel, if I'm going to do anything at all, I'm the kind of person who gives 110% or I don't do it."

I do understand what people are saying when they make that statement. But, all too often, it's yet another thing people say, it's like the perfect non-answer, and I rarely have ever seen the people who make that emphatic statements give it any %, much less 110.

"Let me get back to you. I'm the kind of person who likes to do my research."

Again, I really do appreciate this answer. But my response to them is always, *"Great! Let me get you the compliant and up-to-date information from the company so you can accurately make your decision. What things in particular do you want for your research?"*

People go home and Google the company or they ask their armchair quarterback buddies what they think. Viola! They have their answer, and that answer is generally whatever popped up in the *"research"*. It's always better to make sure people have correct information to review. They deserve to have the right information because the wrong kind may steal the benefits of the products, and the potential of the opportunity from them. In my experience, people rarely ever actually go home and "do research" to the extent they say. So, make sure they have the right information to look at. Their opportunity may be at stake if you don't.

18. SOCIAL MEDIA GAMBLING

I f you are the one who occasionally posts on social media, then sits watching and waiting for likes and comments to pop up, hoping that someone will message you wanting to be your customer or join you, I'm sorry, but you're just not going to see the results you want. I know this strategy and all the mental activity feels like you're going somewhere, but it's more like the gerbil running on the wheel. It sure feels like we're doing something because of all the emotional energy it takes to finally hit post. But this is **NOT** the only or the best way to engage.

Maybe you strategize about how to word your post, thinking that will give you an edge. Two grueling hours later, you hit post! On and on it goes, with a refresh here and a refresh there, waiting for someone to message you. You were even told that liking, commenting, and friending lots of people is the key to building. Nothing wrong with that. Yes, do all of that, but do it because it's genuine, not because you're lying in wait to pounce and hit them with your deal, which if that was the ONLY reason you liked and commented on their stuff in the first place, you're wasting your time.

MANY people are taught to friend and connect with people with the intention of pitching them their opportunity. Sadly that will not produce what they think, and it will hurt the reputation of your products and opportunity.

They believe with this tactic they can build their business effectively, so after weeks of friending, refreshing posts, endless scrolling, and looking at what everybody else is doing, They shut down and think this just isn't for them. They either start badmouthing their company, quit, or just jump into another deal.

What about you, have you been trained this way? People want REAL, people want GENUINE, and people need a real CONVERSATION.... I dare you to try THAT instead of gambling on social media thinking that if you keep rolling the dice it will eventually happen for you. Activities and strategies like that never duplicate or create beautiful teams, they only create attrition, and turn off a lot of people to our industry. **THIS IS NOT** how to operate in network marketing!

This is a business, and if you treated your current job with those kinds of tactics you wouldn't last long. If you operated with that kind of mentality on a job you would be incredibly frustrated because of the mess it would create, and end up hating what you did, and if you weren't fired you would likely quit.

So why do we treat home-based businesses in such a neurotic way? I want you to succeed, and I want you to see this nonsense for what it is. You can be reconditioned to win, but you have to do it right, but if you have never been shown how to do it, then all too often it's the blind leading the blind, and that is why so many fall into the ditch in network marketing.

All my years in network marketing have taught me how to do it **wrong** and how and do it **right**. I really hope you're feeling a bit lighter by this point in the book and begin to see that you're not crazy. We all go through this junk, and, to a large degree, my success is because I have made many adjustments all along the way over the years after making all kinds of mistakes. I never chose to allow my misses to define me, and I'm confident you won't either.

19. TEN PENNIES, A SMALL PRICE TO PAY

A business man went to work each day with ten pennies in his left pocket. He had a rule that he couldn't turn off his work day until he had put all the pennies in his right pocket. This was a physical reminder and measure he used to build his business. When he left his house each morning, he was on a mission to talk to ten people every day. He would explain briefly about his company, the products, and the opportunity, and how they could be involved if they had an interest. He would not go to bed until his mission was complete. Every time he had a conversation, and made sure he got someone's information so he could follow-up, then and only then, he would take one of those pennies from his left pocket and transfer it to the right one. That simple plan after a while made him a fortune in his company. His success caused people to ask what his secret was? He shared the method he used and explained how easy it was to do as that it kept him mindful and on task. He said, "I see people everywhere I go. The pennies simply remind me to actually talk to them!"

I can hear the pennies jingling in your pocket now! You know what? If that will make you do the income-producing activities of sharing and following-up, then go find your pennies.

My suggestion is that you don't measure your success and the results only on a daily basis. Watch how that daily activity translates in a month or three months from now, then take your temperature. Remember planting the seed is only one part of the harvest process. We all feel defeated from time to time, but all too often we shut down if we look out and don't see green fields at the end of 24 hours of planting. There is still a process to get the fruit. Be wise, be patient, and don't set yourself up to fail by expecting harvest overnight.

Getting your products and opportunity in front of one person at a time starting now, can actually cause others to experience the lasting fruits of your labor many years, decades, or even to the next generation if you treat your opportunity seriously. The beauty of network marketing is that it's not always and singularly on you. You tell a few. They tell a few. They tell a few. They tell a few, and the magnitude of what that can turn into is astonishing. A little done daily over time can turn into a lot for your tomorrows.

Earnings are based on personal activity and leverage. The amount of products moving through your organization will create the check. The more leverage you have. The higher the earnings, and the more lives that are changed.

Quit spending your energy trying to motivate your teams. It's EXHAUSTING! Motivate yourself to action instead. People will follow, but it has to be their choice to do so. You're can't want it for them. Your job is to create an environment in which they can be motivated in, but your main action is to get your product and opportunity in front of people. Whether you create a little, a lot, an empire, or fail miserably, it's all intentional. Take total personal responsibility for the results you are getting. That is the first step to victory. After you have the success, do what you want, but, if you want more than hobby money, put your head down and work your business daily without fail!

20. A LITTLE CLOSER TO HOME

If you find there's not a lot of agreement at home, and your family or spouse is giving you resistance, I get it. I know some of you have very challenging circumstances in trying to build your business. Sometimes the resistance is legitimate, sometimes they're just not listening, or maybe they are even threatened by your potential success, crazy I know! My advice.....quit trying to convince them. Close your mouth. Put your head down. Stop talking about it, and build your business! There's not a $5000 residual check that can't cure even the most disgruntled spouse. That's how it was for me.

When Holley saw this thing starting to pay off, she was a believer, but not until then. She was scared and *couldn't* hear about what I was doing. Why? Because it was 2008 and things were a mess, and we were pregnant with our second little boy while she was working in lending, so to cope, she had to shut it out. She just did not understand network marketing or being an entrepreneur. I knew that she was just unfamiliar with this model, so I didn't bother talking about it much at all. **She was focused on keeping a roof over our heads and I was focused on getting her out of corporate America!** My focus allowed me the mental freedom to not have to wrestle anyone, and I brought her home in just under a year after I started with my company. She had a very successful career in mortgage banking, but it was all consuming, and she came home every day exhausted. So when I got her out, she NEVER looked back, and hasn't ever since! She was never mean, controlling or criticizing of me, and she trusted me implicitly. She simply didn't understand what on earth I was doing when I would leave the house every day and tell her, "I'll see ya later. I'm going to go make it happen."

Our situation was fairly simple. We both agreed to focus on what each of us did best, and that created an incredible life change for us, but it's not always that smooth for people. On occasion, we have people in tears sharing with us what a hard time they were having because of the literal hell that they deal with from family as they shared their opportunity with them. Sometimes there is so much control that even going to a meeting or training is almost impossible. They cry on the way to the meeting and wipe away the tears before they walk back in the door. I really do understand. I'm not telling you to pick a fight or just do it anyway, but I am saying that we live in a world of relationships where silent control, manipulation, and verbal emasculation are not uncommon and almost always are the result of prior conditioning. People are broken, hurt and fearful. Hurt people, hurt people, and fearful people place fear on others. I'm so very sorry if crazy stuff like this is going on in your personal life. The path to freedom is never easy, but it's worth more than anything when you reach the other side! Even though the illusion of a giant canyon seems to be between you and your freedom, when you cross it, there will be many tears of joy, renewed vision, restored relationships, and a renewed passion for life.

When you see people living completely strangled by circumstances, you won't just pass by them the same as before. Whether they are the up and outers, the down and outers, college kids, retirees, people who need a little financial lift, or people who really need a financial life preserver. You'll be reminded that *your* freedom can be an example they can anchor on to, so they can believe for their own freedom in life.

21. BUILDING A BUSINESS IN YOUR MIND

Are you building your business in your head, or actually talking to people?

That question changes the game and is the timeless measuring rod for how you should operate in your business.

So, I'm asking you now: Are you actually talking to people, or building in your head? The answers I get vary. Most of the time I get, *"Well, I shot out a post on social media this morning."* So, then I ask again, *"Are you actually talking to people?"* (meaning your companies story, the products offered, the business opportunity, why you are doing it, and the ways they can be involved).

"Well, I went to the office supply store and bought a bunch of

folders, a stapler, a printer, some ink, a dream board, and a new computer."

"Are you actually talking to people?"?

"Well, I went to a coffee shop and set up. Just so you know, I'm trying to prospect, but I didn't really see anybody I thought would be good for it."

How much did you say you wanted to make again? How much do you need so that you can go part-time at your current job? How much do you need so you can quit, and actually pursue your dreams for a change? Nothing gets done until you share the story with people. It has got to be held at the top of the list as **THE** most important thing you do on a daily basis. *EXPOSURE, EXPOSURE, EXPOSURE!* The people who are making the most money in this industry are the ones who are personally getting the products and business in front of more people. Some use social media like a giant vacuum drawing people to them, and some are relentless about regular meetings and gatherings, there is no magic! Yes, there is an occasional person who gets "rich" because a superstar explodes underneath them, it happens all across our industry, but you cannot train from that vantage point, nor should you! No not build and train your teams using anomalies as the standard or the norm. Even though it does happen on occasion, you will frustrate people by avoiding using organic disciplines as the REAL method to grow.

What can be built organically, and grown by the average person, is what should be trained on, be-

cause THAT is duplicatable, and THAT is real.

Do you know what a "chicken list" is? The term chicken list is a list of all of the people you are too "chicken" to share your product and opportunity with. They are the ones who you generally respect, you believe are successful from what you can tell, are too busy (you think), don't need extra money (you think), and would probably never do it (you think). But if you could "get them with their contacts", WOW, your business would pop, right?.... just being real here, we've all thought it.

People have the tendency to reach out to the most broke, most needy, and most desperate people they can think of. Why? It feels good. It's easy. It's safe to "reach down". Hey, I have been down, and I had people constantly approach me with things.

I tell people to write down the most successful business people they know because many times they become your champions! And you might be suprised how willing they are to help. (that is if the opportunity being shared is solid) I've even told people I'm reaching out to them because I was too chicken to ask them to consider being my customer or join me in business. You would be amazed how much people love to hear that you were chicken of them. They're surprised and flattered at the same time.

Remember that successful people who understand the power of residual income are not afraid of it! To those with that success mindset, hearing about residual income is like listening to a heavenly tune, they may even start to drool and start tingling all over. You know why?

Because every wealth model on the planet comes from a leveraging model. Through the mechanism of people or technology, money and time create a residual effect. The exponential result of 1 hour eventually producing 100 or 1,000+ hours of productivity is their language!

Make your chicken list, and speak to these successful go-getters first, not last. If you talk to all the "needy" first, they'll exhaust you, and at that point, if you survive it, you may be to afraid to speak to the people that really have the mindset to actually do it. Companies don't try to convince people to work for them, they interview and pick those that would best benefit their bottom line. **THINK LIKE A BUSINESS**, because you are one…. and not a psychiatrist. Really dig deep and ask yourself how many new people you have put your products and opportunity in front of. If you're not seeing your business grow like you want or need it to, the easiest thing in the world to do is to get choked down by the idea of more training. Don't fall into the trap of thinking that if you could just get your team motivated, or if you just trained them more, your business would take off.

WARNING: Consistently exposing your products and opportunity to people is what will cure any ill that could be thrown at you, not endless trainings!

22. GOT BOUNDARIES?

*Do you have hours of operation
in your business?*

We all love to preach about the potential of having a full life with time and financial freedom because of our opportunities right? Of Course, that's the underlying hope and the one of the core reasons this industry is so sought after. The wisdom in using many hands to move enormous weight is brilliant! Whatever freedom means for you, it's all relative, and only you can determine what that means. It does in fact happen for those that decide to not be derailed, and press on consistently regardless of how long it takes. Their breakthrough will come in time if they don't quit **AND** continue to do those income producing activites... it's incredible, and worth it!

Yet all too often people end up trading an old kind of busy for a new kind of busy. It turns into a 24/7 consuming weight that is always on them. That does not sound like freedom and nobody is looking for that!

One way to stay free, is not to always be thinking every second about building your business, you still have to enjoy your life. You don't want to take a multitude with you from an old busy to a new busy. Having hours of operation is paramount, healthy, and **NORMAL** in the real world, so why not adopt the same discipline here? When you find yourself reacting every time the phone rings, every time you get a social media alert or message, every time team members need you to speak to them and answer their questions, you're setting yourself up for exhaustion. This will create a personal distain for your business and *that* will actually end up repelling people, even if you don't feel like you're throwing that vibe off. You're creating a team of consultants who will be eaten alive with non-stop reactive behaviors, which will cause burnout. Help them, yes! Answer questions, yes! Do it all, but do it within your hours of operation, and then **TURN YOUR BUSINESS OFF!**

What About You?

It's time to reward yourself! It's about recalibrating and detoxing from feeling overwhelmed. What do I mean? Turn it off and do something for you!

In talking to peers in the industry, I was stunned to find out what an extraordinarily high percentage of people do not have a healthy outlet to recharge, especially because this business is *supposed* to make that possible for them. A lot of people find themselves consumed with building the business in every conversation, thought, and angle of their lives. I enjoy asking the people I know in the business what they do for fun. So, I'm asking you, too: What do you do for fun? Does everything under the sun have to have a business agenda attached to it? Should every social media post be orchestrated for your online lifestyle campaign? No! And it better not be. It's not healthy, and it can actually work against you. Why? Because people are savvy, and they'll see through it or they will be pressured by it as a way to operate. And both things go back to what we talked about earlier — repelling people, and creating a Frankenstein.

Back in the day your credit score was what people used to decide your value. Today what you are like online does! You should absolutely take every advantage of and use social media. In today's world, we live online. Your business presence should be there. I'm talking about being consumed with it to the point that you're actually becoming plastic because you are always on a mission to promote your personal branding. Nobody wants to meet or follow a plastic robot.

Take a break from the promoting and the posting and think about what you do for fun. What's your hobby? When I was a kid, I was big into riding motocross dirt bikes and then street bikes as I got older. As a kid, it was such a beautiful freedom to be in the wind. It was my outlet. Even as an adult, I'm able to do everything else in my life more effectively when I take the time to do what I enjoy. No agenda, no social media posts about it, just riding, or hiking, or exploring a new town and dining at a new restaurant, walking the beach and dreaming together, or shopping for things with my wife that are just for us. Some just have a glass of wine at a painting class for a few hours to recharge. It doesn't have to be big folks, but it has to be done. Find SOMETHING where you are *present* and in the moment.

> People don't join a network marketing opportunity because they are looking for a new kind of busy to replace their old kind of busy, so don't set that example for them to follow.
>
> ~ Gabriel Sedlak

Having an outlet is one of the key pieces to having a healthy network marketing business. When you can no longer do anything, think about anything, or act on anything that is not related to your business, you are in a dangerous place.

People don't join a network marketing opportunity because they are looking for a new kind of busy to replace their old kind of busy, so don't set that example for them to follow. Remember most people are in jobs that only allow small windows of time and breaks for people to live. They are not interested in the same crazy. They want to be free from that, but how many examples are there out there of people that are actually free and living a life they would trade theirs for? Not many!

You need to have an outlet to re-calibrate and just get away from it all with your family or by yourself. Do it for you now and those following your example will thank you later.

Yes, you do have the time. You do! You can build this business from anywhere, at any time, on any beach, in the car line, or at night before bed! Do you have any idea how many hours a day people look at their phones and scroll, or waste time in general? I believe the latest statistics for phone scrolling is about 3 hours a day! You could build a HUGE business in network marketing if that time were used there instead, and actually be paid!

I want you to find an escape every week. Maybe it starts off with a couple hours, then a half-day, then a full day. Work into it. Extend grace to yourself. **Everything you need in life to have a breakthrough is already inside of you and in your control.** The panic, striving, and all the anxiety that drives us to never rest is what makes us sink, classic quicksand scenario. The scripture speaks of the fact that in all our laboring we are to *strive* to enter into rest. That sounds like a paradox, but even surrendering to gain control is often the only way to survive and thrive. The most powerful forces on this earth are paradoxes. Give to receive an increased return. Serve to gain the true power to rule. Die to live as with a seed.

I heard a story of a family years ago on vacation at the beach when one of the older children went into the surf and was overtaken by the waves. In a panic, the family rushed up to the water's edge, screaming for someone to help. None of them could swim. A lifeguard began to run as fast as he could to the boy. When he reached the water's edge, he stopped and refused to go into the water. The boy was flailing, thrashing, and kicking violently, trying to keep his head above the water. When he finally couldn't keep up his strength, the boy went under, came back up, then went under for a second time. At that very moment, the lifeguard exploded into the water. In seconds, he had the life preserver around him and pulled him back to shore. While there was rejoicing and cheering from most everyone, the family of the boy was angry and crying. They all rushed the lifeguard and demanded to know why he waited as long as he did to save their son! The lifeguard said calmly, Ma'am as violently as your son was kicking and swinging his arms in panic, and as big as he is, if I had gone out to get him while he was doing that, he would have pulled me down and would have risked us both drowning or being seriously injured on the rocks right under the water where he was thrashing. I had to save both of us.

Now apply that you your business. There's a real parallel here. We thrash and we kick every second of the day. In panic, we strain, try to make lists, come up with all kinds of strategies, attempt to reinvent the wheel, plan to plan, and assume every outcome beforehand with every person we haven't even spoken to yet. If and when we allow ourselves downtime and the breathing room to be coachable and submit to the processes already in place, **THAT** is usually when growth starts. *Resting is how you build a huge organization.* I didn't say lazy, or inaction....

Wrap your business around your life and not your life around your business. Forget the list of things to do to the house. Forget the errands. Forget all of it for just a minute. It will be there for a later time, I promise!

~ Even the hardest steel has to rest and cool between heating and pounding. If not, it will break when needed most.~

I was guilty of not having boundaries. At the end of the day, on more than one occasion I would be so exhausted from all my craziness, my wife would say, *"Babe, you haven't said a word to me today."* I was so busy with others, thinking in my own head, and constantly reacting to what I thought were *"immediate"* needs that I honestly thought I had been having extensive conversations with her. Crazy, I know! I've been so mentally exhausted after days of "busy work" that the computer would slide off of me onto the floor while I was lying in bed working because I fell asleep. I've even fallen asleep on conference calls speaking to my teams' prospects. A new busy for an old kind of busy. Remember that you joined your opportunity to get free from that. Watch out! It will **NOT** produce what you think it will. If every time you see somebody post you feel like you have to look at it. Every time you see a new message you can't help but click on it. Every time you see someone in public, you get wild eyed waiting for the moment to start the conversation about your opportunity, **STOP,** this is another reason many have been turned off by this industry. These knee-jerk responses cause us to constantly be in the mode of business, which is the opposite of what is intended. The *really* sad part in all of this is that you might not actually be present. You may have even retired from your former career. You may be with you spouse and kids, but are you truly present when you're with them? I sure hope so.

There were periods of time before I had boundaries that my wife and children suffered more than they should have because of this. They say to me now, *"Dad, don't worry about it, we don't even remember it, we understand and understood then,"* but still I hate that it happened, because a lot was missed. There was never rest. Anxiety was all over me to do, do, do, without the sizable results to show for it because most of it was in my head. It stole countless hours that I can't get back. Some of you would say that's the price you pay for success. I disagree. The world tells you that, but the farmer understands it differently. When his fields are growing, and he is resting, he understands that he has tapped into the power and potential of the seed when it is placed in good ground that was tended to properly.

> What's worse than not being around working a job away from the ones you love all day, is being around, but not being present.
> ~ Gabriel Sedlak

There will always be times of busy work, but there is always a paced order in which to gather the harvest. Done out of order, your harvest will rot.

A gentleman who has made many millions in our industry and helped countless companies be successful, pulled me aside years ago and told me I should set specified hours of operation for my business and limit my availability, and that people need to earn my time.

He said,

"I suggest doing what I do. It's worked for me, and I think it's a good place to start until you fine tune it to fit your life. The world won't end because you're not jumping at every little thing. As independent *consultants, you must become system dependent, not personality dependent, have hours of operation, turn your business on and then turn it off, for your sanity, for your family, and for the health of your team to be able to duplicate."*

Wow, did I need that! I needed it badly, but I really did have a hard time hearing it. It took me a few years to actually do it. I even had to get sick and broke out in hives for a whole year from stress to see what was going on because I was so strung out "building". I wanted you to know, I'm not just writing what I read somewhere and copied from others. I'VE BEEN THERE!

23. WHAT YOU DO NOW IS SHAPING YOUR FUTURE

When you think about your future, what do you see? What do you see yourself doing? How well are you living?

For example, if your company has a car program, have you cut out pictures of the one you want? Have you been to the dealership for a test drive? Do you have a video of yourself sitting in the car telling yourself that this is the car you're getting?

How about going by yourself if you're just starting, or taking your team out to lunch, and then all heading to the dealership for a dream and drive together? Talk to the management at the dealership. Let them know what you all have as goals and what vehicles you are all shooting for. A dealer would be nuts not to make your experience and future visits with your teams welcoming and exciting. Let that synergy create a collective excitement and use it as an excuse to get your team together. It becomes a great place to bring new consultants to as well. These "remember when" moments dreaming together are some of the best glue you can use while you and your team are pushing personal limits and going from milestone to milestone.

Step out first! It's like preparing a baby's room with furniture and decorations before your sweet little one arrives. You're expectant, and so you act. Faith and vision act first, not after the fact. The powerful stuff in life is always reverse engineered. Win first, then do the work. Don't wait until you have everything and then add on when it makes logical sense. **This is why so few do anything**. They wait. We were created to be like God, having vision and seeing, then creating what we saw.

You have to expand your vision and then it gets filled. Obviously, the car program is not the end all, be all. But applying these truths in every part of daily life makes the super important parts of life easier to conquer. Something like a car program is a simple step to greater future victories in other areas.

It's not just a car bonus you're working for, it's **ANCHORING VISION!** It's the future you're creating for your family. It's a necessary stepping-stone as you progress toward the higher things. Let the skeptical family member, friend, or spouse ride in it with you after you get it. The conversations about your products and business have a tendency to be a far more positive one at that point!

Was money a motivator for me? Yes! You better believe it was! Why would you work any job if the money didn't have a dominant part?....Say this out loud!

"Money and time were created to serve me. I was never created to serve money and time!"

I have had nothing several times in my life, and I have had something, even a lot of something. I much prefer having a lot of something! I have been at the bottom of the barrel. I've lived in my car(s) on more than one occasion. I got ready at gas stations, took showers at apartments clubhouses, soaked in hot tubs to treat myself in the cold weather. With this time I turned it into opportunities to read books that forced change in my mind as I got more and more free with every page! I've slept on people's floors. I've had to totally rebuild my life from zero on a couple occasions. There's always a story behind every success story. We are all just a few breaths away, or a few dollars away, from everything changing. You have to be victorious before you get the stuff, and then when you get the stuff it's properly understood and used. If you lost the stuff, then getting it all back isn't hard, because of the way you think. Even when I lived in my vehicles, or was smack in the middle of contrary circumstances, I never allowed those circumstances to define me, even though I knew other people saw me and my circumstances as the same and measured me accordingly. I knew it was simply a temporary state, that it would not last forever, and that it was not me or my identity!

When I was struggling, and it may seem like a little thing to some, but I always knew that one day I'd be able to take family members with me to Disney. To pay for extra rooms, food, and everything necessary to make the Disney magic really come alive! I always knew we would be able to sponsor children and help to provide for their needs all over the world. I always knew that we would be able to sit down and spend extended amounts of time to dream with people who no longer had the

capacity to dream. The dream house, and dreams cars, yes, those great too, and I love that part as well, but money is simply a tool to create more leverage, give you more options, and give you more time back. *That* should make you eager and excited to work hard to get more of it! Or even, *a lot more* of it! You'll then start to paint your day as you wish, not as you need. When was the last time you were in charge of you and not ruled by all of the demands put on you by everyone?

Having the freedom to be independent and to enjoy your journey in a special way that is tailor-made for you, *that* is what it's all about. *Time* is the new rich!

We aren't forced to live in a particular place because of work or school. We master the clock. We master our calendar. We have designed our lives on purpose to never miss a moment. I'm trying to give you the gift of hope and possibility. Use our example and go build it bigger, better, and more efficient than we have....PLEASE!

24. YOU JOINED... REMIND ME WHY?

I sure hope you didn't join your business because it felt like the thing to do at the time or because it was easier to say yes than no to the one who shared it with you. Maybe you finally gave in because you were approached so many times? Were you bored and thought you'd give it a shot? How you start, and the mindset you have when you start, is everything and sets you up to a large degree for how your business will play out.

I hope you joined because of great products that can really make a difference in people's lives and for the potential of adding a little extra or maybe even a lot extra to your bottom line.

I don't *ever* apologize for personally gaining, because I offer somthing of real value to people.

I wanted to set my family free financially, and what that

> You shouldn't feel uncomfortable about making money when someone buys something from you of value. No company on earth apologizes when someone buys what they're selling.
>
> ~ Gabriel Sedlak

meant to me is what drove me to run with it to the degree that I did. Why create frustration for yourself by playing with it, and being apologetic?

Now if all you want is a few bucks here and there, fine. There are many who choose that path in our industry, in fact most *will* take that path. And that is perfect for them!

But did you know it's actually easier in life to succeed at things than it is to sit on the edge, be lukewarm, or fight against it? Someone once said, *"If you play with network marketing, you'll get play checks. Work it seriously, and you'll get serious paychecks."* I like that, but wait, let's apply that to any job, the same is true.

One way I relate to success and the fruit that comes from it is because of how school was for me. I did so terrible! I saw how the teachers related differently to the students with the good grades. From the students' side, they were more self-confident. School itself was easier, and there was a beautiful progression with things, a sense of pride. From the teachers' side, there was a healthy communication between them and the students. They always beamed with pride when they said their prized students' names. They would ask the kids to lead the class on occasion, assist them in tasks, and on and on.

Then there was me. I rarely did my homework, hated even going to school, was made fun of, and would profusely sweat because I was so self-aware and nervous that I smelled. My nickname was "Smelly Sedlak." I smelled like animals because we had so many cats and dogs in our home growing up. (That's a whole other story) The teachers always corrected me openly. I back-talked the teachers, was not reserved about my opinions, was in the principal's office regularly, had notes sent home, skipped school often, and had conferences requested with my mother from the teachers. The bullying and pressure from the other kids and their opinions of me made school hard. *Very* hard. What I fundamentally thought of myself was not much. I retaliated by being a smarty-pants and acted like I didn't care. But, *oh*, I really did care. I was trapped, and everything in the school setting worked against me. I never did finish school, but I did eventually got my GED in my twenties. If I had it to do over, I would be a straight-A student for sure, knowing what I know now. Actually, I would home school and be an entrepreneur from a young age. There is nothing cooler than that, and why we do it now with our kids! When you choose to succeed in life, everything has a way of working in your favor. I sure wish I knew that then.

Do the right things now

Do the right things now, and over time most things will work in your favor. The company will recognize you. Your income will increase. You will be respected by your team, and people will start to seek you out and want to be a part of your team. **(Of course you'll have your haters, but they will do more to promote you than your**

fans will!....that's a bonus!) That's a big shift, from trying to look for people to share your opportunity with to people now looking for you! That is one of the *big rewards* of going after your opportunity aggressively no matter what.

In the music business, if you write a hit song, suddenly everyone wants to write with you. Land a big role in a film and suddenly everyone is calling you wanting you to be in their next movie. Score the winning touchdown in the game and suddenly people want to interview you, even if the whole game you sat on the bench before that one play.

Have you noticed all the new personalities popping up on social media? Seemingly small in the beginning, then they're speaking at conferences and events across the country. Then suddenly they're **THE** go-to in a particular field. **THE** person that everyone now thinks of.

Success breeds success. People champion people who are running, and *that* is why you must run! It truly makes life more fun and *far* easier to succeed in the future.

WARNING: I highly suggest you choose now how you want people to relate to you. They will relate to you, but how they relate is totally in your hands.

25. DON'T ASK FOR A VOTE

You don't need to over-plan, and you don't need to ask for a vote. What do I mean? Say you're going to schedule a product overview and opportunity meeting or video conference in a week for you and your team to invite prospects, You start reaching out to everyone to let them know your plans.

"Hey, what day works best for everyone to meet up? I'm putting together a gathering for folks to hear about the products and the opportunity."

Mistake. The question that you should be asking yourself is: *What works best for me?*

You're a leader. Lead; they will follow. If you build it they will come. If it's valuable to them, they will make the time or they will when they can in the future.

Set the date. If it's important enough, people will make it. Thirty minutes before the meeting begins, you start getting text messages. One after the next, people cancel.

Sometimes it's legitimate, but many times it's not a priority yet because of the lack of value they have for it. The time comes for you to start the meeting, and two people show up. You invited 45 people. You start the meeting late waiting for more people to show up, which made the ones who came on time feel not as valuable. You opened the meeting with,

"I invited 45 people, and I guess it's just us tonight, let's go ahead and get started, thank you for coming. I'll make it quick this evening because there is just a few of us. Maybe next time we will have a bigger crowd."

Sound harsh, it is, but I have heard some variation of this more times that I want to remember from people, especially in the early stages of them growing their business.

Yikes! You just killed the meeting and made the people who did attend feel insignificant. You imprinted on them that you are not someone they would want to join. One person buys a few products. The other one has to think about it and ask the spouse then fell off the earth. Sound familiar? Whatever you do, pick a day, follow through with it, and don't apologize no matter who does or doesn't come. Make the people who showed up feel like the most important people on earth, because **they are** during that moment!

I have seen over and over again, one person showed up and was treated like the most important person on earth. Guess what? *That* person became the next million-dollar or multi-million-dollar earner in the company, and some have gone on to be the top leaders, speakers, and authors in our industry today.

It takes so much energy to get a vote on everything you are planning to do. Operating like that will make it hard to even want to continue building because you'll start feeling like it's too emotionally exhausting to run your business. You'll start to play out what your future meetings will be like in your mind, and you'll shrink back instead of move forward.

Nobody needs a few weeks to plan if something is important to them!

People impulsively do things all the time if they want to, and are excited about what they want to engage in.

People will tell you they don't have the time. Wrong! They always have time for the Netflix binge, the constant scrolling on social media, the constant complaining for hours with their friend about how they just don't have time and how much things need to change. The truth is that if people don't see value in what you are offering, they won't make the time or spend the money. People do what they want, are as busy as they want to be, and buy what they want.

> "I don't have the time"
> "I don't have the money"
> "I am just way too busy"
> These are the classic three knee-jerk responses that have stolen more dreams from more people than anything.
> The truth is, people do what they want to do, buy what they want to buy, and are as busy as they want to be, for what they are really interested in. Opportunity waits for no one, protect yourself from yourself, and do it anyway!
> ~ Gabriel Sedlak

26. BUT I LOVE MY JOB

What if you could still pursue your passion, but you could do it for free, without the schedule? You say you went to school to be a nurse, and it's your passion. That's wonderful. I'm not telling you to stop. What if you could go and volunteer as a nurse offering your services for free? You didn't have to deal with the politics of the hospital, all the drama, and the grim reality that you have to observe every day? You wouldn't have to be on your feet 16 hours a day. You could pick the type of people you wanted to work with because you're free financially enough to do so. Extra money allows you to still be a nurse. You can even go part-time. You can also nurse people back to financial, emotional, and physical health. Nursing is a gift, not a job you do.

See, it's not that you have to quit being a nurse. It's about the *gift* of being a nurse. It's something you carry with you everywhere you go. Does nursing mean working next to a hospital bed every day, giving meds, doing your rounds, and all the other countless demands? No! Nursing is about having a passion for people, and I want you to think outside of your career and think about the gift itself that you can use in life anywhere you are.

What if you're a teacher by trade, and/or have kids of your own? You have spent years teaching other children, but now you want to teach your own kids and not miss any more moments. What if you didn't have to work every night grading papers, and you didn't have to try to cram all of your free time with your family within just a couple months of the summer? What if you could be a teacher, could volunteer, and not have to deal with the politics of the school system and the social restrictions and demands of the political climate that steers your ability to really teach the kids in a healthy way? What if your gift was operating outside the classroom? The gift of being a teacher is very different from physically teaching in the classroom. I'm not saying give it up. I want you to think about how, where, and at what level you could teach. Teaching outside the confines of a *job* enables you to tap into the gift and the passion of it in a far bigger way.

What if you're a corporate recruiter and you're filling spots for executive placement, the medical field, healthcare, or IT? You're good at it, and you love people! You are constantly going to meetings, have quotas, pressure, expectations, and all the time clock demands. It's turned your passion for people and helping them to get a job they love into seeing them as dollar sign, and you hate it. You're traveling all the time and spend long hours away from your family, but you didn't realize in your wildest dreams that you could use those skills to build an organization recruiting for *you*. Doing something like that could provide residual income, something you don't currently have for your family. Heck you could actually build your business from the beach! Do you currently have a job that creates passive/residual income, that can be built from *anywhere*?

You're talented as a recruiter. You've been a rainmaker for everyone else. Why not be a rainmaker for you and your future? Nobody is going to fight for your freedom and future like you will! I want you to think out-of-the-box and think outside of your job. Whatever your talent is, whatever your skill is, it's a gift that you carry inside of you. It can be applied to any arena in life — especially network marketing!

> ### *You don't have to simply punch a clock and do a task at a job for a paycheck.*

You already know how to do what you do blind-folded. Why not apply those same skills, same gifts, in a network marketing model that literally has the possibility to change the trajectory of your family forever? **Did you know that working is very expensive?**

> *"You don't buy things with money, you actually buy things with the hours of your life." ~ Jim Rohn.*

It's *very expensive* to give your time anywhere other than to you and your family's future. No matter how good you

> You don't buy things with money, you actually buy things with the hours of your life
> ~ Jim Rohn

are at your job, unless you are in control of your money, work for yourself, and have money and time working for you, then you are actually disposable if you work for someone else. That is a level of risk that will never go away as long as you are an employee.

People tell me all the time that they could never do anything they didn't absolutely believe in so they're only going to do what they know and like. I get it! But I'm trying to get you to think bigger than that limited logic. I want you to think about investing your time and talents in things that really make a difference through leverage.

If you look at any successful model that really creates wealth, time, and financial freedom, they are always leveraging models. It is used as a tool, regardless of whether or not there is a deep emotional affinity to the vehicle.

For example, a man speaks to his investment advisor and his advisor tells him there's a cat food company that has really shown huge numbers and he's been tracking it for a while, and has even personally invested money himself.

Because of that the advisor tells the man he thinks it's a smart move to invest in the cat food company now. The man doesn't understand. He doesn't even like cats. He tells his advisor that he's going to pass because of his distain for cats and that he only invests in things he likes and is interested in. *What?!*

No one would never say that. If the numbers are good, you invest. Period. It has nothing to do with "liking it" necessarily. It's not about being "in to" cat food or cats. It's about a wise business model. You invest where the money works for you, you have leverage, and where it's most profitable. Obviously, as one who invests you want people to purchase vast amounts of cat food, fishing lures, carpet, automobiles, etc from the companies you invest in, but being *"into"* those things profoundly yourself is not a requirement to make a wise investment.

Allow me to share my personal example. When I got into my opportunity, I knew the reputation of the founders, the products, and their prior track record. Their success was unprecedented in the space. It wasn't really up for debate. My initial intrigue was that I could share their story and didn't have to be the expert, they were! Having a super profound connection with the products in the beginning was a progressive thing as I began to understand them more and see personal results. My progressive connection did not change the fact that what they were offering was solid, whether I joined or not. Because of my history in network marketing, and because I saw what a company with incredible products could become, I was thinking business. You see, I knew that the products offered an emotional and very profound answer for a multitude of people. I had to warm up to them, but that did not stop me from seeing the business model. The funny thing is, in the beginning I saw the business, and my wife loved the products. Then after a short while, I fell in love with the products and my wife fell in love with the business.

I love cars, and I have some nice ones myself. I have always loved going to different dealerships to look at the latest models. When I go I always ask the salespeople which model they drive. Some drive what they sell, and others don't, even though they work there. If they tell me they work there because it's an incredible brand, and that they actually drive a 1990 pickup, would I believe that I couldn't buy a car from them? Of course not! They are representing an incredible brand that has a proven track record. A salesperson not driving one personally doesn't affect the brand in the slightest, if he properly represents the brand. They are working there to feed their family, whether they adore the brand or not. Do you see all these crazy angles of logic are just not valid arguments when making a purchase or over-thinking about a business venture?

Any pain, discomfort, disconnect, or warm up time that may be there when you start your opportunity, will actually start to go away as you begin to get your feet wet and engage. Even if it's not ultimately your passion at the current time. Stand tall and represent your products and opportunity proudly, knowing that a multitude *will* buy them, and will buy them from someone. So why not you? I write like this to encourage you to begin to treat your business like you would any other career, because you already know how to *that*, and this industry shouldn't throw you for a loop or spin you out.

I have seen people jump into opportunities at the same time several other of their friends did, only to over-think it and wait to really connect emotionally. They gradually test the waters here and there to make absolutely sure people will openly embrace it when they share it with them. But that "testing" is inaccurate because of the wet noodle posturing they have when sharing. They have no real skin in the game yet, so they are not committed at any real level and can always walk at any time, so their *exploration* time is not an accurate guage. They sit back and allow the *"ideal time,"* the *"epiphany"* to appear and if *that* magically happens **THEN** they will decide to engage.

Meanwhile, the others who joined at the same time decided to be consistent and treat it like a job, do the work and get it in front of people. They go to a completely new level in their pursuit of time and financial freedom. The first one continues blaming people and circumstances for the lack of change in their life. They end up digging deeper into their current career, go back to school, get more degrees, or pursue another "greener grass" opportunity which promises they can be "first" and get in on the "ground-level." Meanwhile, their peers in the first company were consistent, treated it like a job, went part-time, or maybe have even retired from their prior jobs by that point.

Some get better, and others get bitter. Have you been the person I just described? Do you blame the company, your upline, or your downline. I know what I'm talking about! I see it all the time, and it's a *miserable* way to be. Don't you dare continue like that! Shake that destructive self-sabotage mindset off. Extend grace to yourself and re-invent yourself today. How? A decision. Remember nothing on this earth is more powerful than your ability to choose. *That* is where your power is — choice.

Don't allow what you do, what you are really into currently, are super passionate about, or what you were educated in, to blind you and keep you from the leveraging an opportunity in network marketing. **It's a business at the very least, so don't treat it like it's not.** You are a messenger, not the message. You already know how to work, which you are likely doing now for a company to feed your family and keep a roof over your head. Whether you currently get tingles every time you walk in the door of your job now or not, you continue to do faithfully what pays you, right? Since you already know how to work, then my suggestion, is for you to allow yourself to work this industry the same way until you have the freedom to pursue your dreams with abandon. Allow the network marketing model to set your family free so you can finally do what you really want. That's what I did, and I treated it like a real job, because it is, and a fun one at that!

27. LEAVE THE DRAMA FOR THE THEATRE

L et's talk about the crazy stuff for a minute. You may or may not have experienced anything in the following examples, but I know that some of you have. Because it's not always the easiest to navigate through, I decided to write about it here to help prevent you from being burdened by it.

Inevitably people will come and go from your opportunity. You may start with one company and end up joining a few before you find *the one*. I have been in several companies over the years, and would move on for one reason or another as well, just like with any other career.

As an independent consultant people are "free agents" to come and go as they choose. The critical part to understand so that you're not stressed out by the things you can't control, is that you are ultimately **only responsible for you** and **what you do** in your opportunity. You are not responsible for your team, for their performance or lack of it, and they **don't** work for you. If they take the business to the moon, fantastic! If they build a little here and a little there, fantastic! And if they move on, then of course you wish them success, which I hope you still see as fantastic! They are independent consultants after all. Getting **that** settled in your mind in beginning is critical!

Now to be a bit more specific. It can be tough when drama happens in your business, but you **CANNOT** allow the actions of others to rob you from your momentum or keep you from moving forward. There are all kinds of opportunities people will be presented with along their network marketing journey. Some opportunities when they are presented are simply more ideal for them, and when they go to a different company, they do it with integrity. They let everyone know they have decided to move on, wish everyone the best, and are thankful for the time they had. On the other hand when some people move on, they create a far more messy situation.

Network marketing like any other type of business that involves people will inevitably have some drama along with the victories. I want to adress the drama briefly for one reason. So you are prepared mentally when it comes. I want you to say, "Oh yeah, I remember reading about that in the CUT IT OUT book!", and not be shaken by it.

Let me give you a few brief examples:

I've had people join us in the business, and after we've poured into them, they quit, and join someone else in our company.

I've had people who joined, got all the training and re-sources they could, with the intention of only using it to build another opportunity in another company. As soon as they got what they needed, they quit and pursued the new one.

I've had people that were already in another company only join ours to cross-promote in order to fill their other one with customers and consultants from ours. This occurs all over the industry and we shouldn't be su-prised. Wait a minute, this stuff happens in the corporate world as well, not just network marketing.

I've had people tell me they were going to change the world and then they dropped off the earth. One time I was at lunch with a super excited consultant who was a respected business leader in the community. She was so excited about the possibilities, she could barely hold her excitement back! We had a great conversation discussing all that she was going to do, and all the people she had already told about the products and business that were interested in hearing more! Then suddenly after about a hour chatting, she looked at us, excused herself to go to the restroom, and never came back to the table. We still have no idea what ever happened to her?

I've had people join and quit three times, but on the fourth time of joining they run and build a BIG business! Was it a bit frustrating, sure, but every time they came back we treated them with just as much respect and ex-citement as the last time, and supported them just as much. People carry a lot on their shoulders and you may never really find out what's going on behind closed doors. They simply need to be encouraged when they step out, because when they do, *that time* could be the one that changes their life forever.

A few more points on the subject of drama and sowing discord:

When people are building their business in a particular network marketing company, then are almost out of the blue suddenly ready to jump into the latest fad of the week that comes knocking, they often make decisions in haste and don't ask the tough real long term questions. Usually because they are blinded by shiny object syndrome, and the promise of greener grass...... in other words they see *money*. Unfortunately you will find that some choose to go after people from the old company to fill the new one by speaking negatively about the company, products, leadership, their team, or something else derogatory about the old one. They often will do both for a while while they are filling the new one. Their zealousness and short term foresight actually does far less to serve those they are reaching out to than for them personally. If the opportunity falls apart, they just jump into a new one, but those that were pulled away from their original business many times never regain their momentum. Does it take two to tango...YES, but people are led away by words, and those words plant doubt, and that doubt muddies the water and prevents them from seeing clearly. People don't realize that sowing discord hurts families, incomes, and tears apart organizations. It's more common than you may think, and so sensitive and potentially damaging that people don't know how to handle it when it happens. I have watched organizations paralyzed and stop growing because of the size of the exodus and the back biting happening behind the scenes. The drama and choosing loyalty between the companies and relationships scrambles the follower to the point that they don't recover. Whatever could have been in network marketing is lost, and they leave the channel all together.

I remember a group of about seven or eight consultants all in a row that joined a company around the same time. They had massive synergy together, people were joining and becoming customers in droves, and because of that the money was really becoming incredible. One of them who helped spearhead the movement was led away by another opportunity that popped up, but all the others stayed the course and became millionaires. The one that left couldn't even look at or talk to the others anymore because the company they jumped into fell apart and they were so sick about the decision. Over the years they joined a few other opportunities.... they are still looking for what they lost.

Everyone in our industry is an **independent consultant** and can choose the path they want. But come on folks, someone needs to talk about this stuff. It's real and has caused a multitude to quit our industry!

If I can gird you up and get your head strait, and talk about the challenges that may arise, then if and when they happen you won't be suprised. Your resoluteness of mind and your decision to take total ownership of **you** and what is **produced** will simply allow you to see it as just a speedbump in a parking lot, you slow down for a second, go over it, and continue on your way.

You needed to hear what I just wrote. Does it bother me that those kinds of things happen? It use to, but honestly at this point in our career, I am more sad for the people that get sidetracked more than anything. I really do want them to succeed, and people can go to a better opportunity if one arises, definately. But knowing that this kind of drama comes with *life*, it shouldn't paralyze us or cause it to eat at us. It happens, and when it happens, we just press forward, because where we are going and where **YOU ARE GOING**, *that stuff* cannot go with us.....Human nature is everywhere, and is not removed from any enterprise.

Over the years I have watched these kinds of things happen so many times I can't even count anymore. Having been in this industry as long as I have has given me a lot of experience with all the craziness of human nature, including my own! I have put myself through so much unnecessary junk, and I gained nothing of real value from it. Some would say experience, but honestly wisdom learns from others, but the foolish always have scars from frivolous battles.

> Sometimes the cupcakes make your stomach upset, and sometimes the roses prick you, yet they are still delicious, beautiful, and so worth it.
>
> ~ Gabriel Sedlak

Every success story and every company whether in network marketing or not has this as a backdrop somewhere.

You may have had some of this drama happen to you, you may have watched it happen to others, or you may be the one creating it.

As I said in the introduction, don't slander your team or your company. Stay in your own lane and build with integrity. If a better opportunity reveals itself, fine. But there doesn't have to be a trail of carnage, broken friendships, and torn apart organizations in its wake. Folks who operate like that end up burning bridges, wandering from deal to deal, lonely, and with few real friends. I know it's tough, this journey hasn't always been cupcakes and roses for us. Yet here we stand.

28. ASK THEM TO DANCE

This reminds me of the quote I heard from H. Jackson Brown Jr., "Opportunity dances with those already on the dance floor." Building your business is a lot like the high school dance. You know what I'm talking about. The dance in the gym where all the guys end up hanging out on one side, and all the girls hang out on the other side. They all talk about who they'd like to dance with, but they're all too scared to ask anybody. If you're at that dance two things could happen. One: You stand frustrated the whole night and never ask anyone to dance. You beat yourself up badly on your drive home because you'll never have that chance again. Two: You ask the one you really wanted to dance with and find out they had hoped someone would ask them to dance. Now *that* drive home is a very different kind of drive!

As you got onto the dance floor, all fear left you and a sudden bravery hit several of the other boys. They too now had the courage to ask someone to dance. At first, you were the crazy one. But when the whole school is on the dance floor, guess who the weird ones are now? The ones still standing on the sidelines watching.

I promise you that's the way life works. When you are the aggressor and make the first move you might be really surprised to see what transpires because you were brave. Confident people are just more attractive and have more followers.

In your business, you have people who have watched every move you've made for years, but they still after all this time haven't joined you. You need to ask them to dance! You need to grab their hand and let them know it's safe. Directly reach out with a personal call, note, or private message. They will be relieved, even if it takes a few reach-outs for them to respond. They see it, and they are thinking. Some people really need you to make that move because they won't, even though they secretly really want to dance.

29. WITHOUT SALES, NOTHING WORKS

Let's talk about sales for a minute.

Y ou hear it all the time: *"I'm not a salesperson." "I don't want to sell anything." "Do I have to ask my friends and family to buy stuff from me?"*

I want to help all of you embrace a different way of thinking about this. **Nothing on earth happens without a sale!** Every minute of every day you are a part of it. Take a car, for example. The leather on a steering wheel was sold by a supplier. The supplier bought it from a grower. The grower had to buy the food from a feed company or a farmer to feed the cattle that produced the leather. The leather was sold to a curing agent who prepared it to be used in manufacturing products. The leather distributor sold it to a car manufacturer for the interior, the seats, the dashboard, the trim, and the steering wheel. And did you know there is a paycheck and a family provided for on the other side of every single sales transaction along that process.

If sales were observed under a microscope, and every stage was a stronger lens, you could zoom into the sales process infinitely and realize how connected and complex it is. We could literally go through the entire world, point at every item, and trace the sales process. Your ability to survive and exist is because of sales. Isn't it about time we became non-apologetic and embraced it? **SALES IS LIFE!**

So, do you have to sell anything in network marketing? Yes! Yes! Yes! and Yes! And be glad you do because if it's all about "signing up" as the main focus, and the products are not the main focus, and there is not a sale of a product at every level, you better run away as fast as you can!

Do not be ashamed of sales. It is how the world operates, and you are deeply involved in it every day of your life. I am getting hungry while writing this chapter and will need to go eat something that was sold to me with money I made selling things while I sit at my kitchen table that I also bought from someone that sold it to me. This morning we had groceries delivered. Guess what? All of the ingredients in that stuff had to be sold to manufacturers and then to distributors who then delivered it to us.

How do you change your financial future? Sell a lot of stuff to a lot of people through a network of people and you'll get a little piece of a lot of sales. Again, that is how "traditional" companies work but in network marketing, you get to benefit.

We have done extremely well for ourselves over the years in network marketing, but we didn't get any of it separate from sales. Be proud of sales. I know I am!

30. USE WHAT'S IN YOUR HANDS

There are a lot of reasons people are successful in network marketing. Some people are just better connected and better positioned than others and see success easier and sooner due to the network they already have. *There, I said it!* Somebody needed to, and what's wrong with that? They earned those connections, and connections to people is how the world goes round.

Some people are just social media machines. Some people have incredible social circles. Some wear yoga pants every day with a glass of wine in one hand and are incredibly influential in their communities. Some are big in the country club scene and are always at charity events and social gatherings. Some are pastors of churches and their position creates the ability to lead people at many levels. Some own businesses and are very influential. Some are professional or ex-professional athletes and have maintained great relationships within those circles. Some are celebrities who will always have followers. Some had years with other opportunities and wherever they go they have a mass following because of who they are.

But letting **ANY** of those examples create the idea that you can't be as successful as they are unless you have "what they have" is harmful and wrong. You can totally be successful, but you have to do it your way, with your personality, with your frame of mind where you are at the moment you start. You have to do what you can with what you have in your hands right now!

The common thread in each of these examples is that these people have cultivated a community. When they join an opportunity, they are able to tap into those circles because of the trust, notoriety, or their history with those people. You may have heard the saying, "Your network determines your net worth." Welcome to the real world! There is a *big* element of truth to that.

But — and I mean *but* — we live in a time like no other time in the history of the world. A 16-year-old can create a personal brand with ten million followers using a cell phone! A young woman can post her outfits and have 250K followers because people are drawn to her style. Using his phone, some guy can film himself working out and create a national movement because of his passion for fitness. Someone can throw hundreds of pounds of fruit loops into a swimming pool, it goes viral, then suddenly sponsors appear. And yes, even a guy like me with no real formal education, a very challenging background, no one to really help guide me in life, with many critics and naysayers along the way can become very successful in network marketing. I say this to encourage you, that whatever you want in life is within reach, if you want it bad enough.

Do likes, views, and followers make you money? Maybe, maybe not. Companies look for people with audiences more than talent these days. Noise and eyeballs seem to be the new currency. Those who make the most noise — influencers — are sometime compensated very well. But for long-term sustainable success, you need to provide something of value. *Real* value. There has to be a product, or a service regularly purchased somewhere. For the consumer, money is given when perceived value exceeds price. If what you are offering is valuable to someone, price is rarely an issue.

Another group that is held up on a pedestal are the people who explode, seemingly out of nowhere. The top earner of the week. The flavor of the month. The personality of the day. There is always a story behind what you see, *always*! Do remember that the world celebrates people who perform and have the results to show it.

No not confuse the following statement as a get rich quick or a loose just throw your business cards around idea, but because you never really know what people are going to do with opportunity when it is presented to them. I know of people who dropped their business cards off on a restaurant bulletin board or at a casual run-in, and their lives were forever changed by the one who picked it up and the organization that grew because of it. Or someone gave their card to someone at a drive-through, or casually in the monorail at Disney, and had their business explodes because of it. What a blessing! Please remember my family's life was radically changed because I received a phone call from a friend! **A PHONE CALL!** Do not think that even the smallest touchpoint doesn't have power, because it **DOES!** Consider how many musicians had a video loaded up online and just the right person saw it, and things changed for them forever because of it. Or someone got on one of those talent shows and finally their gift was seen by the world, and *that day* everything changed for them. Not talking lottery here, you just really never know *who* or *what* is going to change your world. Remember the ABCs of our industry: Always Be Chatting.

I don't train or encourage people to wait for their magic moment, and I am fully aware that true grit and consistency is how success almost always happens. I just want you to be expectant that every seed you plant matters, because what comes of it can be bigger than what you may have originally thought.

Let's say a private jet manufacturer hired a new salesperson. A super personable 26-year-old young man landed the job. He went to a coffee shop on his *first* day off just to catch up on things. As he sat there, he struck up a conversation with a kind and friendly gentleman there with his espresso-colored miniature poodle. It's a lighthearted conversation full of laughs and dog stories. The young man is a dog lover too and grew up with miniature poodles. The two men shared the crazy antics that particular breed is known for. After about half an hour, the dog owner looked out the window and noticed a 1966 Ford Mustang and asked if that was the young man's car. The young man said it was and asked the dog owner if he wanted to come outside and check it out? He replied with a resounding, "absolutely!," and shared that he had a car just like that growing up. The young man threw him the keys, and asked when was the last time he drove one?

After returning from a spin, with a smile from ear to ear, the dog owner turned the conversation to business and learned that the young man was a salesman selling both new and preowned private planes. As luck would have it, the dog owner owns a private jet executive leasing business and is looking to add five additional planes to his fleet. Now, what do you think could possibly happen because of this odd run-in at the coffee shop? Yep! The young man landed the sale of those five planes and is immediately respected and lifted up within his company and is asked to train all of the other salesmen.

Obviously, this is a hypothetical story, but business like this is done everywhere, every day, from lunch meetings, to golf course and coffee shops. Does the company immediately create a training manual on how to go to coffee shops and speak to dog owners? No, but that is exactly what seems to happen all the time. People try to create a packaged formula, and training following anyone's specific success.

What do you think the responses will be from the seasoned salesmen when they hear about this new "young buck?" A lot! The reactions to the success of others drives all kinds of responses. Those who do just enough to keep their jobs act one way. The hot-shots in the company act another way. The heroes of last quarter also respond in a certain way. And still some rejoice at his success and are thrilled that he made the sales because they understand that it helped the whole company. **For the young salesman, it's critical that the back-story is shared in**

detail so that it encourages and demystifies the success rather than frustrates the other salespeople. You want the salespeople to grab hold of it and realize they, too, have a chance to do something bigger than what they may have previously imagined, if they just decided to be personable and talk to everyone they meet, because conversations change to business all the time. By openly and honestly explaining how and why the success happened, humility and encouragement are fostered within the organization, rather than frustration and jealousy.

Sudden success may in fact happen for some of you, but be careful that you use it to make a bridge for others to cross over.

You are accountable for how you use the success and platform given to you and how honest you are with the back-story. That's not a burden. It's an honor. Do not allow jealously and comparison to create an emotional undertow that will hurt your business and your team. By sharing the true back story, you actually save people the pain from creating their own version of how they think you did it. **Top leaders struggle with this all the time, and would avoid a lot of drama, and see even more success if they were willing to pull back the curtain.**

People have a hard time celebrating others openly if they

are secretly envious or jealous of them in private. Some people seem to work far harder and don't see as much success as some who seem to work far less. Remember, a lot of that stuff is your own perception. You don't know what's behind the scenes and how hard someone worked to get where you perceive they are. Getting successful is one thing, but staying successful takes work. as it has been said,

"Don't judge another mans public harvest, you don't know the seeds he planted in private".

You will have magic moments all through your organizations if you stay the course. No matter who you are, what your background is, or what your circumstances are, you can be successful. Consistent, daily, income-producing activities will make up 99% of your successes. I'll say it again: Expose the message to new people, and use the ABC's (Always Be Chatting).

Do you think if the young airplane salesman in the coffee shop story was quiet and kept to himself, things would have worked out differently? Yes! Whatever you do, DON'T BE SILENT, EVER!

Scrolling on social media for ten hours a day, comparing yourself to everybody else's success stories is not an income-producing activity. Follow those who inspire you, sure. But don't waste your day having hundreds of images flash before your eyes without action. That will defeat you before you start.

31. OUR WAY OF BUSINESS MAY NOT BE THAT EASY FOR SOME

I know professionals from various backgrounds who have made a ton in other careers but can't seem to get traction in network marketing. Many will blame our industry for that or believe that the business model is faulty at some level. Since they can't get it to grow, something must be wrong. Over the years I've observed a few common threads with many professionals that join network marketing companies, but don't see the results that sometimes people far less qualified than them tend to have.

* They try to reinvent the wheel.

* They think they have a better method, and exposing the opportunity to new people is replaced with preparation and training overkill.

* They treat their team as disposable rather than seeing both their team and their customers as **THE** most important part of their business.

* They have a boss/employee hierarchy mentality, because they are the upline, they think they're the boss.

* Or a BIG ONE is, because of their business pedigree and degrees, somehow network marketing is beneath them.

All of those classic tendencies are conditioning. If there was one word to describe our amazing industry it would be, **INTERDEPENDENT!** There is so much power in that word, and whether up or down the line, everyone's actions affect everyone else's results. It fosters a servant posturing by everyone on the team. When that is the culture, nothing is impossible, no matter where they are in the organization!

Our business model is worth fighting for and needs to be shouted from the rooftops! Sometimes a corporate mindset can prevent people from getting their head around the idea of powerful residual income. In the corporate world, a predetermined wage is attached to a job, skillset, or degree. But guess what? That wage also has a limit. If someone in network marketing makes $5K $10K, $25K, $50K, $100K++ a month or more, it's baffling to many, and quickly dismissed.

Now if a CEO, CFO, doctor, professional athlete, musician or celebrity makes it, nobody says a word, it's actually held up high and praised.

Someone may be thinking, Yeah, but don't most people

fail in network marketing? OK, I get the question, no, actually most just sell a little and make a little. No failure there, that is what they chose to do. If you are speaking of BIG success, then I have to say that most people fail at everything BIG. They fail as golfers, real estate agents, racecar drivers, navy seals, actors, artists, the music business, as songwriters, in marriage…. goodness, and in every other endeavor under the sun. The problem is NOT network marketing, it's people. People fail at everything. But why does the failure of others have to predetermine what YOU will do, and what YOUR results will be…**IT DOESN'T**.

A corporate mentality many times tells you that no one can make more than the owners or the higher-level management. How do people who come from a deeply ingrained corporate mindset, value, fight for, and join the "field" that may very well make more than *them* or the *owners* regardless of their education? Generally, they can't. Instead they come in with a mindset of trying to run it like a traditional company and go into management mode with their teams, or just dismiss network marking as a sub-par business model. Big mistake! That is other big reason many people fail. They have not settled in their mind that this industry is a legitimate business model. Because of that doubt, they are never engaged fully, and they still carry an apologetic edge. You can't apologize for your business! It will never mature into anything that way. A company will let you go in a heartbeat if you're not adding to their bottom line. Heck, even if you are adding to the bottom line, you can still be let go suddenly!

The "traditional" business model has armies of people

who have mastered getting up in the morning. The alarm clock is their drill sergeant, they accept their wages, do their job, and deal with corporate politics. If they are passed up for raises, they deal with it. If their holiday bonuses are lost because the corporation didn't make some goal, they deal with it. They have to punch in and out for lunch, have limited breaks, miss ball games, dance recitals, etc. Nobody argues against it. As a matter of fact, it's seen as normal. And I am not against that, if that is what someone chooses. And I am fully aware that many have been totally fulfilled and have created the lives of their dreams through it, and I applaud them for it. I just want people to hear there may be something else out there, something they maybe aren't aware of that could provide the freedom they are looking for.

Because working for a traditional job cost so much in education, sacrifice, time, and exertion it's seen as *valuable*, must be fought for, and thus legitimate work. And because anyone can just walk in off the street and join a network marketing opportunity, it's many times dismissed and seen as suspect. People build their lives, get in debt, buy homes, cars, choose schools, revolve their entire lives, banking on the fact that their jobs will last. With everything in life there is always risk, network marketing is no exception. But on the other hand, it gives you an *incredibly high level of personal control*, allows you to increase financially as *you* choose, and allows you to do it from anywhere on the planet at any time.

For me, it was having my wife and kids by my side every step of the way, and NEVER missing a moment in life with them! And since the the day I took network marketing seriously, I've never had to!

◆ ◆ ◆

WARNING: "Opportunity" always looks suspect to those who feel they are stuck.

32. NOTHING HAPPENS ALONE

Remember we have a business that is interdependent. You're in business for yourself but not by yourself. The size of your organization will determine the level of financial freedom you have. An organization with $10M in monthly volume is going to pay you differently than an organization with $10K in volume.

Network marketing is you having a simple conversation, that can turn into a business, that can spread all over the world, and *you* get to benefit from the growth. It happens through a network of people sharing through a decentralized army of happy customers and consultants. I would rather have 1%, 2%, 3%, 4%, or 5% of 1,000 people's efforts than 100% of my own. What about 10,000 peoples efforts? What about even more? I just want you to think BIG for a minute, because that is **EXACTLY** how companies see it! That is how wealth is created! Banks knows this. Real estate brokers know this. The music industry knows this. The investing world knows this. The company you work for knows this. Every restaurant franchise knows this. The stock markets know this. And yes even network marketing opportunities know this. Isn't it about time that you have leverage instead of simply being leverage for someone else? Network marketing can give you a life that is so far beyond anything you've ever allowed yourself to imagine.

The pitfalls, warnings, snares, tendencies, and destructive mindsets shared in this book are not uncommon to people. Those of you who now see them for what they are — thieves, monsters, social rhetoric, indoctrination, lack of self worth, wrong theology, conditioning, and self-sabotage! — will have no problem extending personal grace to yourselves, then **IMMEDIATELY** and **AGGRESSIVELY** grabbing your sword and cutting them out of your lives to take back what is yours.

It's an honor that you took the time to read my book. I hope you feel like you could run through a wall right now, because of the weight lifted off of you, and that you're not crazy! In fact you are now beginning to think normal.

Use the sections and the points I wrote about with your teams, refer to them as often as needed to recalibrate when things go awry. Please be sure you reach out to us and share about your victories, and what you cut out to reach them!

Blessings on you and everything you touch. May your family be forever changed. May you fight for the freedom to pursue all that is in your heart to do. May your children see you only as a champion in life. May your victories shine bright illuminating the way for others to follow. And most of all, may you realize that what you needed for your breakthrough was inside of you all along.

Mark **this day** on your calendar as the day that everything started to change for you, because **today** you decided to finally **CUT IT OUT!**

Here's to your incredible future!

~ Gabriel